BLOOM'S BEST
PERENNIALS
AND GRASSES

Photographs by Adrian and Richard Bloom

Adrian Bloom

BLOOM'S BEST PERENNIALS AND GRASSES

Expert Plant Choices and Dramatic Combinations for Year-Round Gardens

Timber Press
Portland | London

To my wife Rosemary, who with this book, as in life, has helped and supported me throughout.

Foliage and flower make a dramatic combination in the Summer Garden at Bressingham. The golden yellow leaves of the dogwood *Cornus alba* 'Aurea' form the backdrop in late summer to the taller-growing *Miscanthus* and *Eupatorium* *maculatum* 'Gateway' (left) and the tawny plumes of *Cortaderia selloana* 'Patagonia' on the right. In front from left to right are *Perovskia atriplicifolia* 'Little Spire', *Sedum* 'Herbstfreude', *Echinacea purpurea* and *Agapanthus* 'Premier'.

Text copyright © 2010 by Adrian Bloom. All photographs copyright © 2010 by Adrian Bloom and Richard Bloom except those appearing on page 11 (bottom) by John Friel, page 36 (bottom) by Marcus Ryan, page 37 (top) by Rick Darke, page 62 by Christopher Grey-Wilson, page 89 by Juliette Wade/GAP Photos and page 134 courtesy of White Flower Farm.

Published in 2010 by Timber Press, Inc.

The Haseltine Building
133 S.W. Second Avenue, Suite 450
Portland, Oregon 97204-3527
www.timberpress.com

2 The Quadrant
135 Salusbury Road
London NW6 6RJ
www.timberpress.co.uk

Designed by Dick Malt
Printed in China

Library of Congress Cataloging-in-Publication Data
Bloom, Adrian.
 Bloom's best perennials and grasses : expert plant choices and dramatic combinations for year-round gardens / Adrian Bloom ; photographs by Adrian and Richard Bloom. -- 1st ed.
    p. cm.
 Includes bibliographical references and index.
 ISBN 978-0-88192-931-7
 1. Perennials. 2. Grasses. I. Bloom, Richard. II. Title.
 SB434.B488 2010
 635.9'32--dc22

2009041288

A catalogue record for this book is also available from the British Library.

Contents

How to Use This Book

Perennials and grasses are for everyone. Regardless of your level of experience, and whether your garden is big or small, this book can help you find new plants to enjoy all year round.

These plants are remarkably versatile. With careful planning, in combination with others (especially woody plants), they enhance the garden with flowers and foliage throughout the changing seasons. Through the photographs in Chapter 1, I have tried to demonstrate their year-round appeal in our gardens at Bressingham, where each seasonal transformation brings richness and drama.

In designing our gardens, we all need inspiration and I hope you will find it in Chapter 2, which highlights the use of perennials and grasses in often stunning (and always thought-provoking) gardens and landscapes around the world.

When it comes to plants we are spoiled for choice today. For some years, I have been trying to simplify gardening and find a way to give new or inexperienced gardeners a better chance of success; "less is more" is, after all, often a truism. In Chapter 3 I put the spotlight on twelve reliable perennials and grasses that, when used together in myriad combinations, will hold appeal throughout the changing seasons.

All plants have a history and an origin that can, once explored, add knowledge and interest to the experience of gardening, and on a practical level offer insight into the conditions they need. This idea is discussed in Chapter 4, along with information on how to choose from the seemingly endless assortment of perennials and grasses available today.

Chapter 5, which sets out the practicalities of preparing your soil, buying plants from the nursery, planting, lifting them, dividing them and cutting back, may be the least glamorous chapter, but following the guidelines will help you get the most satisfaction out of your plants.

In the Directory, I feature and recommend some of my favourite perennials and ornamental grasses. In order to give more information on some of the best and most reliable options, I have gradually narrowed the selection to what I consider to be the best performers, all of which have stood the test of time on both sides of the Atlantic. The Directory gives a description of each featured plant, as well as historical information, practical advice and other recommendations.

This book is not intended to sit on the coffee table, although if you find it there, I hope you will pick it up and leaf through it. The photographs are intended to inspire, and their captions to inform. I would of course be very happy should this book move you to put your gardening ideas into action, and to relish the satisfaction that these wonderful plants can bring to the year-round garden.

The best perennials sometimes need seeking out. The hardy *Geranium* BLUE SUNRISE 'Blogold', seen here at Bressingham in midsummer, was discovered by Dutch plantsman Hans Kramer in 1992. It has a long period of interest from golden, red-tinged buds and early growth to soft golden yellow summer leaves, the colour held even in some shade, and a good long display of lavender-blue flowers that re-bloom freely into autumn.

What Is a Perennial?

Most perennials will grow and flower each year, maintaining a live but dormant rootstock (subject to cold and heat tolerance), in contrast to most annuals, which grow and produce flowers and seed in the same year before dying.

A herbaceous perennial is essentially a non-woody plant that grows each year after dying back in winter. As always, there are exceptions to this rule; some perennials retain their evergreen foliage until the following spring when new growth begins. These plants, including *Helleborus*, *Bergenia* and *Epimedium*, provide a longer period of interest—especially when their leaf colour changes from green in summer to an intense purple-red or ruby in winter, as is the case for some bergenias.

A hardy perennial is one that can be expected to survive and thrive for several years in the area where you live and garden. Of course, the definition of a 'hardy perennial' can become complicated because soil, aspect, shelter or exposure can all determine hardiness and success in growing. The opposite of hardiness, but equally important when selecting perennials and grasses for your garden, is the factor of *tolerance*—of extreme heat, drought and humidity. Some non hardy perennials can be treated as annuals and grown for one season.

Preface

This book has been a long time coming. It's been 50 years since I started working with perennials, and 43 since I began planting up our garden, Foggy Bottom, with conifers, heathers, trees, shrubs and other plants. Since childhood, perennials have played a big part in my life. It took a while, though, for me to become passionate about them.

My father, Alan Bloom, was a perennial nurseryman and plantsman who started the Blooms nursery in 1926 in Cambridgeshire, England, before moving to Bressingham, Norfolk some 20 years later. By 1955 Blooms was among the largest perennial nurseries in Europe, and around that time my father turned to developing his first island beds of perennials at the front of our home at Bressingham Hall, gradually expanding his garden to six acres.

Upon finishing school at 18 I was enlisted to help, spending some months on the new garden and established nursery, but I found it less than exciting; at that age, the prospect of joining the family business held little appeal. Instead, I set sail for the United States where, after a short spell at a Maryland nursery, I worked as a tennis instructor at a Vermont summer camp, a janitor at the Winter Olympics at California's Squaw Valley Ski Resort, and finally an unsuccessful encyclopedia salesman in San Francisco. Somewhat demoralized and not sure of what I wanted to do, I decided to return to England for Christmas 1960 and give horticulture a go.

In 1961 I began working at the famous Frikart nursery on the shores of Lake Zurich, Switzerland, and the following year (after a winter speed skating in Norway) I spent five months at the perennial nursery of Poul Petersen in Denmark before returning home at my father's request to our perennial nursery and farm in Bressingham. With my brother Robert initially managing the farm, we began over the next few years to develop our wholesale nursery, which grew rapidly with the developing garden centre market and gardening boom in the '70s and '80s, adding conifers and shrubs to the range and promoting new plants under the Blooms of Bressingham name while also developing a successful retail mail order business under the title of Bressingham Gardens.

As the name of Alan Bloom was becoming synonymous with perennials at the time of my return, I focused instead on developing conifers and promoting them throughout Britain, writing books on the subject and planting a six-acre garden of my own called Foggy Bottom. But increasingly I found myself working with perennials, combining them with grasses and woody plants for year-round interest, and selecting those that were reliable, long lived and with a long season of attraction. Thanks to help from my wife Rosemary and other gardeners over 40 years, the six-acre garden in front of our house at Foggy Bottom continues to evolve, with perennials and grasses now playing an ever more important role.

While in Britain I had been known as "The Conifer King", in North America my name was decidedly linked to perennials as I spent many years promoting and planting them throughout the country. In partnership with some leading nurseries, a new company, Blooms of Bressingham North America, was formed to distribute perennials to American gardeners. To inspire the public to learn more about our plants, following an example I had first tried

← Our garden, Foggy Bottom, in 1982. Started in 1967, the 6-acre garden was initially planted primarily with conifers and heathers to give year-round appeal. In early spring, winter-flowering heathers are in bloom.

↙ Foggy Bottom in 1999, with new plantings of perennials and grasses against a background of trees, shrubs and conifers.

out in England, we would "give away" and plant front gardens using perennials and ornamental grasses in combination with other plants to show how they could transform even the most colourless and static gardens into dynamic and vibrant places. The first in Wayland, Massachusetts in 1997 was followed by more in Michigan, Toronto, Peoria and Sacramento and, later, larger and more public gardens in California, Kentucky, Ohio, Long Island and Boston. This proved an invaluable way for me to learn from local experts and see how perennials and grasses performed in the widely varying climatic regions in North America.

Witnessing the enthusiastic reaction from volunteers who helped in these mostly one-day planting programmes was immensely satisfying, and their newfound motivation

← I have always been keen to show how perennials and grasses can be used to best effect in the smaller garden. This front garden I designed in Roydon, Norfolk, is only 6 × 6 m (19½ × 19½ ft.)

large, and with the help of garden staff it was cleared and planted in just one day in 1992. Instead of cutting a lawn, why not enjoy the seasonal changes plants can bring?

→
Encouraging people to appreciate, enjoy and be inspired by plants and gardening has always been one of my passions. This garden in Columbus, Ohio had many contributors, from local nursery growers to Ohio State University horticultural staff, Master Gardeners and individual volunteers who worked togther to create and plant a garden in one day. I designed the garden for year-round appeal and in this urban situation it acts as an oasis, with plants softening the hard surrounding landscape. It is satisfying to compare the garden in 2005 before planting [→] to the finished garden just one year later [↘]. Currently it is being used as a learning garden for students.

very rewarding. If we could only bottle up such enthusiasm and distribute it, we would multiply many times the number of people who are motivated to garden.

But over the years, I have learned that inspiration alone isn't enough; successful gardening demands a practical and realistic approach, which means personal involvement, and some thought and effort.

This book highlights the best perennials and ornamental grasses and explains how to use them, but equally it is about the pleasure and benefits, the excitement and the drama that can come from gardening—and often stay with us for life. I hope that this book will show the art of the possible, and that it will inspire you to discover your creative self in the garden.

→
Still enthusiastic at the end of a very hot day in August 2007, volunteers raise their hands, pleased to be a part of developing the new Bressingham Garden at the Massachusetts Horticultural Society's gardens and headquarters at Elmbank, Wellesley, near Boston. Volunteers aged 6 to 93 participated in the day's activities, turning this 1-acre area into a year-round garden.

PERENNIALS AND GRASSES IN THE YEAR-ROUND GARDEN: Through the Seasons at Bressingham

A view from our kitchen window is lit up in late winter by a swathe of snowdrops drifting into the distance. In the foreground are, left, the colourful winter stems of *Cornus sanguinea* 'Midwinter Fire', black-leaved *Ophiopogon planiscapus* 'Nigrescens' and the golden foliage of *Acorus gramineus* 'Ogon', both 'evergreens'. The large-flowered snowdrop *Galanthus nivalis* 'S. Arnott' is regularly divided and planted more widely in the gardens.

Since I began the garden at Foggy Bottom, the key purpose has been to develop year-round interest using a variety of plants, so that the garden is just as colourful in winter as it is in summer. Back in 1967, evergreen and deciduous shrubs (including heathers) and conifers were used to fulfil the winter role while perennials and the few ornamental grasses grown at that time were usually all tidied up and cut down before winter began.

But then over time I started planting more perennials in the shaded areas where heathers would not succeed, and in the mid 1980s I began using more ornamental grasses that gave a feeling of movement that contrasted with the more static conifers, gradually bringing in more winter-interest shrubs such as *Cornus sanguinea* 'Midwinter Fire', and then planting still more more perennials and bulbs. For the past several years, chainsaws have been used each winter to bring down overplanted and overgrown conifers, opening up vistas and making more room for perennials. Thanks to perennials like *Bergenia* 'Bressingham Ruby', *Ophiopogon planiscapus* 'Nigrescens' and *Helleborus*, winter colour enhances the shrub plantings. Ornamental grasses such as evergreen *Carex* and herbaceous *Panicum*, *Miscanthus* and *Stipa*, whose foliage remains attractive through much of winter, have added immeasurably to our appreciation of what perennials and grasses can bring to the autumn, winter and early spring periods. Of course, perennials come into their own in spring and summer, providing the annual promise of things to come.

The photographs in this chapter tell the story of our gardens at Bressingham from spring to late winter. Admittedly these photos depict unusually large-scale gardens, but try to forget that; many of the plant combinations shown here will also work in small or medium-sized gardens. I hope that you find these images inspirational as you explore what will work in your own garden, considering not only the plants' characteristics but also the impact and atmosphere of the changing seasons.

← As new spring foliage of perennials erupts, the early-flowerers like *Dicentra* 'Pearldrops' nestle the blue-green finely cut leaves, making a long display into summer.

The sharply pointed new shoots of *Hosta* 'Francee' are purple as they emerge from winter dormancy, soon to unfurl to produce large green leaves edged with cream. Springtime is exciting in the garden, as almost daily you will notice change and new growth.

←

One of the most spectacular of bergenias in flower is *B.* 'Eroica', the bronze-green stems holding clusters of rose red bell-shaped flowers, against a hazy background of the pale blue blooms of *Brunnera macrophylla* 'Jack Frost'. Bergenia flowers can unfortunately be prone to damage by spring frost.

↓

Warm spring sunshine quickly encourages new growth. Using sturdy foliage and flowering plants lends a variety of interest to a small space, covering the ground to reduce maintenance demands. From left to right, the brightly variegated *Hosta* 'Patriot' ties in with the green fronds of the fern *Polystichum setiferum* (Divisilobum Group) 'Madame Patti' and contrasts with purple-leaved *Heuchera* 'Prince', as do *Hosta* 'Halcyon', ×*Heucherella alba* 'Bridget Bloom' in flower behind and, in front, the variegated jacob's ladder, *Polemonium caeruleum* BRISE D' ANJOU 'Blanjou'.

←

Persicaria bistorta 'Hohe Tatra', a reliable performer for early summer in reasonably moist soil, is a compact form of the bistort, a European native found in the alpine meadows of the Tatra Mountains in Poland and Slovakia. Unlike *P. b.* 'Superba', which is a rapid spreader, 'Hohe Tatra' is clump-forming.

↑

Midsummer morning light filters through the purple-blue flowers of *Salvia ×sylvestris* 'Blauhügel', an easy and valuable perennial that will flower for weeks.

←

In this moist semi-shady position, perennials, grasses and ferns offer great summer foliage. The large bronzed leaves of *Rodgersia podophylla* fill the background, and *Carex elata* 'Aurea' (also shown front left) provides an erect habit and golden leaves to contrast with the blue-leaved *Hosta* 'Halcyon'. *Osmunda regalis*, the royal fern, is centre right, while the only plant in flower, *Geranium macrorrhizum* 'Album', takes centre stage.

Summer is celebrated by a mass of colourful perennials, soon to come into bloom. *Achillea* 'Terracotta' is excellent in the garden and as a cut flower.

Given reasonable moisture and some shade, astilbes can be spectacular in flower, particularly when given contrast by neighbouring plants. Here *Astilbe* ×*arendsii* 'Brautschleier' is highlighted against *A. chinensis* 'Visions' and the large blue-leaved *Hosta* 'Big Daddy'.

Bees drugged with pollen spend the night in the shelter of the spiky blue bracts of *Eryngium* 'Big Blue', and are still there as dawn breaks. This cultivar has an even more intense colour than *E.* ×*zabellii* 'Jos Eijking'.

↑

The Dell Garden, created by Alan Bloom at Bressingham and famous for its island beds, is awash with colour in the height of summer with six acres planted with around 5,000 species and cultivars. In this bed the tall *Veronicastrum virginicum* rises in the background in front of the scarlet-vermillion *Crocosmia* 'Lucifer'. In the foreground from left to right are brightly coloured *Coreopsis*, peach-orange *Hemerocallis*, the purple-pink spikes of *Penstemon* and deep blue *Agapanthus*.

↙

A mixture of perennials and grasses at Foggy Bottom provides a foreground to the large golden leaves of *Catalpa bignonioides* 'Aurea', the Indian bean tree, which can be kept pruned to restrict size. In front with contrasting foliage and flower are *Miscanthus sinensis* 'Superstripe', *Monarda* 'Violet Queen' (left, and also in the foreground) and *Monarda* 'Raspberry Wine'. *Liatris spicata* 'Kobold', *Kniphofia* 'Percy's Pride' and the early-flowering pampas grass *Cortaderia selloana* 'Patagonia' rise above surrounding foliage at different heights while *Stipa tenuissima* and *Geranium* 'Rozanne' meet the edge of the ground-level grass pathway.

↑

At the height of summer, when faced with a lack of colour, just turn to North American natives like *Echinacea purpurea*; these were seedlings from *E. p.* 'Kim's Knee High'. Other late summer colour comes from *Eupatorium*, *Phlox paniculata*, *Heliopsis* and many more. Now is also the time for perennials of South African origin such as *Crocosmia* and *Agapanthus* to make a show. These are all mixed to create a mass of colour, interspersed with *Miscanthus sinensis* cultivars in the Summer Garden at Bressingham.

↙

With the beginning of shorter days, overnight dew and mists, autumn is nearly here. The morning sun picks out the gold and beige inflorescences of *Deschampsia cespitosa* 'Goldtau' and surrounding seedlings in early morning. This is a glorious time to enjoy the changing 'flowers' of many ornamental grasses, enhanced by the lower trajectory of the autumn and winter sun.

Ornamental grasses add a dramatic element to a more static bed of mostly conifers and heathers at Foggy Bottom in early autumn, none moreso than a river of Japanese blood grass, *Imperata cylindrica* 'Rubra', highlighted by the sun as it meanders through the evergreens. Smaller in stature is *Pennisetum alopecuroides* 'Little Bunny', to the left of the mound of rich green needles of *Pinus heldreichii* 'Smidtii', and rising above centre left is the graceful arching fountain of *Molinia caerulea* 'Zuneigung' which will soon change to golden brown as it goes into autumn.

There is still colour to be had from perennials in autumn, especially from the late-flowering asters such as *Aster* 'Little Carlow', looking striking in the Summer Garden where it contrasts with the foliage of *Cornus alba* 'Aurea'. Behind are the plumes of tall *Miscanthus sinensis* cultivars in varying shapes and colours.

→

The morning sun begins to clear the mist on an autumn day at Foggy Bottom. Colours have been changing on trees such as *Taxodium distichum*, the swamp cypress, in the background. Grasses are at their most effective with the sun behind them. *Miscanthus* backgrounds the erect stems and flowers of molinias and panicums, and below is the purple-leaved 'river' of *Heuchera* 'Prince' contrasting with the white bottlebrush heads of the tender grass *Pennisetum villosum*.

→

Two late-flowering perennials make good company in a position that is shady but not too dry. On a breezy autumn day the waving white bottlebrush heads of *Actaea matsumurae* 'Elstead Variety' are enhanced by the rich blue flowers of *Aconitum carmichaelii* 'Arendsii'.

The first frost of autumn still hangs on the flattish heads of *Sedum* 'Herbstfreude' in the Winter Garden, as leaves of *Cornus sanguinea* 'Midwinter Fire' change to gold in the background. The deep golden leaves of *Molinia caerulea* 'Zuneigung' will soon collapse to fully reveal the silver birch behind.

→

The oak is one of the last trees to shed its leaves, their rich golden brown enhancing the late autumn foliage of *Pulmonaria* 'Opal', *Helleborus* ×*nigercors* and the golden-leaved sedge, *Luzula sylvatica* 'Aurea'.

↑

Perennials and grasses go well together, but work nicely with shrubs too. The seedheads of *Agapanthus* 'Loch Hope' hang on slender green stems, showing up clearly against the autumn leaves of *Rhus typhina* 'Dissecta', the vigorous but attractive staghorn sumach. On the left is the relatively short *Miscanthus sinensis* 'Ferner Osten'.

→

Frost enhances the gracefully pendulous inflorescences of *Miscanthus sinensis* 'Kaskade' in early winter at Bressingham.

23

→

A light snowfall transforms a winter scene at Foggy Bottom, with low morning light creating a magical scene. The structure and foliage of perennials and grasses give some useful winter protection, and seedheads are important as food for birds. Cutting back at Foggy Bottom does not normally start until mid to late winter.

↑

Trees and shrubs can provide colourful bark and stems to stand out against winter snow. *Cornus sanguinea* 'Midwinter Fire' is a must—and it is enhanced by underplanting with black-leaved *Ophiopogon planiscapus* 'Nigrescens', snowdrops and *Bergenia* 'Bressingham Ruby'. This combination graces the Winter Garden at Bressingham in midwinter.

→

The year comes to an end. Visible from the kitchen, this bed is small in scale yet still interesting thanks to the frost as well as the tawny foliage of *Hakonechloa macra*, on the right, still effective in early midwinter. When the new season begins this bed will be cut back and tidied up, ready for the river of snowdrops to come through: turn to the first photograph in this chapter, taken in the same place, to begin another year.

DESIGNING WITH PERENNIALS AND GRASSES

←

In the zu Jeddeloh garden a bold blue 'river' of *Geranium* 'Rozanne' meanders through at ground level, allowing a repetition of a range of plants to accentuate the river effect; *Miscanthus sinensis* 'Morning Light', *Crocosmia* 'Lucifer' and clipped green pyramidal conifer *Thuja occidentalis* 'Smaragd' line the river. This looks like one large island bed but it is crossed from left to right halfway down by a now-hidden grass pathway dividing the two. Virtually any low-growing plant with a long period of interest can be used to create a similar effect. *G.* 'Rozanne' would work well in a smaller garden, too, as would *Heuchera* 'Prince', *Hakonechloa macra* 'Alboaurea' or, in a shadier position, *Ophiopogon planiscapus* 'Nigrescens'.

We live in a garden designer era. Perhaps the glamour and fashion much promoted by the media at events like London's annual Chelsea Flower Show, with its focus on celebrity and designer gardens, started and encouraged this phenomenon some years ago. At Flower Shows we can all admire the professionalism and execution of the best gardens, taking note of our favourite ideas and plants. But as wonderful as these gardens may be, the are built for a single time of year; at the end of the week-long show, they are dismantled. Designing a garden to give year-round interest takes a little more thought and objectivity.

In our own gardens, we have to be realistic. Take a good look at your garden space and decide whether you want to create structure by planting trees and shrubs, or clear away old, overgrown plantings to open up possibilities. The question of soil type (whether acid or alkaline, sandy, loam or clay) exposure to wind, aspect and elevation will have a bearing on your choice of plants. And you may have an idea of which plants (and planting styles) appeal, but—given the size and aspect of your garden—are they likely to fit? Don't overlook the role that plants in containers can play; they provide colour, flexibility and interest that is particularly valuable in very small or urban gardens. You must also consider design questions in relation to the position of your house, how your entrance pathway or driveway is positioned and which views and vistas you can see from your windows: you may want more light in or open views out, or you may wish to have protection from neighbours or shelter from strong winds.

The grand garden designs are often done on a scale too large to relate to most gardens. Most gardeners will want a mixture of plants, in smaller groups, to provide year-round colour on a more limited scale. It is as difficult to scale down a palace or country house estate garden into a suburban-sized plot as it is to plant up an expansive prairie or wildflower garden in a small space, although ideas about plant uses and associations can be learned in each case regardless of your garden's size. In the small-scale garden, dwarf or smaller woody plants and lower-growing perennials can be used for year-round interest.

When designing with plants, aim for a careful balance of structure that can provide continuity yet also change: focal points with evergreens for solid winter form and colour, and ephemeral perennials, grasses and bulbs that can change rapidly to provide seasonal change in foliage and flower. Perennials and ornamental grasses fit in perfectly with woody and structure plants—they are what I call the missing ingredient.

Shapes and forms, such as fastigiate or weeping, add formality and focal points, while hedges provide a background to perennials and grasses, as do foliage shrubs such as *Cotinus coggygria* 'Royal Purple' or *Cornus alba* 'Aurea', which can create striking contrasts. Perennials such as *Brunnera macrophylla* 'Jack Frost' or pulmonarias can light up a woodland setting in spring, as gold or variegated hostas can in summer. The aptly named *Cornus sanguinea* 'Midwinter Fire' has fiery stems once leaves have gone in autumn but the base can be enhanced by winter-flowering snowdrops (*Galanthus nivalis*) and the black-leaved *Ophiopogon planiscapus* 'Nigrescens'.

Experimentation is part of the fun, and some of our

→ A recent replanting was carried out at Foggy Bottom, beginning with the removal of many large conifer specimens that were blocking light from our sitting room. The resulting view utilizes the remaining conifers while also highlighting a large specimen of *Acer palmatum* 'Fireglow' and, centre right, *Acer conspicuum* 'Phoenix' which is here just coming into leaf. Beneath and around these are low-growing perennials and bulbs to add seasonal changes. Early spring finds hostas and heucheras making new growth.

best ideas can be sparked by other gardens. The illustrations and accompanying comments in this chapter show how perennials and grasses are used in the design of gardens around the world. The idea is to open your mind to the possibilities as you consider planning or redesigning your own garden; ask yourself "what do I like, and will it work?" Once you have identified plants that appeal, turn to the Directory for more information on whether they are likely to thrive under your garden's conditions.

Views from our sitting-room window

I believe that it is important to design your garden around your house, so you can enjoy short or long views and develop plant associations that change and hold interest through the year. At Foggy Bottom I am always looking out of the windows from our often-used sitting room, considering how I might improve the view.

→ A summer view from inside the sitting-room window brings the recent plantings almost into the house. A river of *Geranium* 'Rozanne' crosses from one bed to the next to meander through *Hosta* 'Halcyon', *Hosta* 'Shade Fanfare' and *Heuchera* 'Obsidian'.

 ↑

Shortly before leaf fall, both the perennials and the two maples give a good show of autumn colour while *Geranium* 'Rozanne' continues to flower. The conifers, all of which are pruned annually, provide good backdrop, colour and form for the winter.

 ←

Winter snow creates quite a different picture as it clings to the framework of the garden specimens and cloaks the ground.

↑

Part of the massive 128-m (384-ft.) long mixed border at the Royal Horticultural Gardens at Wisley in England, originally planted in the 1950s following a design by noted plantsman Graham Stuart Thomas, is shown in late summer. Judging from the size of the plants from front to back, it is difficult to believe that the ground from pathway to hedge is flat. The fact that it is level clearly demonstrates the capacity for even taller perennials to 'stretch' when close to a hedge or a wall. Most visible in the foreground are *Sedum*, *Rudbeckia* and *Persicaria*, while taller *Miscanthus* in the back is highlighted by the golden-leaved dogwood, *Cornus alba* 'Aurea'. A tall hedge needs tall plants, but this could be scaled down to a small garden by using a much lower hedge (bearing in mind that the hedge will take moisture from plants closest to it). A hedge provides definition, a backdrop, the semblance of outdoor 'rooms' and of course structure in winter. Choose your type (deciduous or evergreen) and prune to your desired width and height.

← For a cottage garden, first obtain a cottage. Well, this isn't strictly necessary—but the area around Richard Ayres's charming 17th-century thatched house in Cambridgeshire, England is an obvious place for a traditional cottage garden, shown here in early summer. It is surrounded by a hedge with grass pathways meandering through mixed borders, which include annuals, bulbs, trees, conifers, shrubs and perennials, an eclectic combination that changes and blends with the seasons in a relaxed but carefully planned way.

↓ Suffolk, England-based garden designer Mark Rumary has overcome the problems associated with planting close to a hedge by creating a brick pathway next to it, giving him two rectangular beds between a central path, with squares of evergreen box, *Buxus sempervirens*, leading the eye and retaining formality. In early summer a variety of perennials show foliage and flower with many, including tall-growing delphiniums, still to come. The far wall, raised pool and twin specimens of Italian cypress, *Cupressus sempervirens*, create an impressive focal point for a relatively small garden. It is very much a garden with boundaries fixed and under control.

→

Formality and informality comfortably exist together in this part of influential British garden designer Tom Stuart-Smith's garden. Low clipped box hedges separate beds from pathways and hold back the relaxed plantings of short-growing perennials, which in turn accentuate the narrow dark green columnar yews,

Taxus baccata 'Fastigiata', that act as a strong focal point all year round. They can be clipped or reduced in height if required. Behind, in contrast to the stiffness of *Taxus*, giving a cloud-like effect with their diffuse and airy flowerheads, are clumps of *Stipa gigantea*.

↓

Informal island beds, created by Alan Bloom from 1953 to 1962, are shown in high summer in the Dell Garden at Bressingham. In the foreground, *Astilbe* 'Straussenfeder' ('Ostrich Plume')

and *Hosta sieboldiana* 'Elegans' make impressive partners. The concept of island beds was a breakthrough, showing how perennials could be grown in walk-around beds rather than

borders. Being a perennial man, my father allowed grasses and ferns but no woody or structural plants were used in the actual bed. An era of greater freedom in using perennials had begun.

↑

Respected Dutch garden and landscape designer Piet Oudolf has created a wide range of gardens in Europe, Britain and North America with almost a trademark selection of mostly summer- and autumn-flowering plants and ornamental grasses, many of which are American natives including some of his own raising. Large weaving drifts—often using repeated plants and interesting textures, with reds, blues and purples dominating while yellow is generally avoided—are also part of his signature plantings. This signature style is evident in a summer view of his design for Scampston Hall, Yorkshire, England with spreading perennials tumbling into pathways, and a delineating formal hedge at the distant boundary. In this garden there is very little structure beyond the erect perennials, which will continue to hold interest into winter.

↓

This natural-looking prairie garden is not in North America; it is in the centre of Weinheim, south of Frankfurt, Germany. Of similar climate to the central eastern and midwestern United States, under the direction of Cassian Schmidt, the plant collection and partly scientific and experimental garden Hermannshof is having a profound effect on European garden designers and increasing their use of North American-origin plants. Few of the prairie plants offer much in the early part of the year, but an abundance of flower, foliage and texture make their show in summer and autumn. *Helenium* 'Waltraut', centre, is one of the first heleniums into flower in this midsummer view.

←

Over to another outstanding garden, designed and owned by Dennis Schrader and Bill Smith in Long Island, New York. Here straight formal hedges and a distant gazebo act as background to the billowing maturing inflorescences of masses of *Stipa tenuissima* as you imagine it might grow in its native Texas and New Mexico. The stipa acts as a waving carpet through which erect, taller perennials can emerge, the indispensable if short-lived *Verbena bonariensis* and *Acanthus hungaricus* (top left) in evidence in midsummer, with agapanthus and others to follow. This idea can of course work on a much smaller scale, too.

←

Can this be England? On a warm summer day with bees buzzing, this garden could easily be in a more southerly location than this sloping, south-facing section of the Lady Farm garden in Somerset, near Bristol, owned by Malcolm and Judy Pearce. Judy terms it her 'steppe garden'. Initially designed with the help of Mary Payne, it uses a clever mixture of mostly perennials and grasses, with the bright yellow flower of saguaro-like *Verbascum olympicum* rising above more lowly neighbours, including drifts of *Carex* and *Stipa tenuissima*. Other plants shown are *Coreopsis verticillata*, *Stipa gigantea*, *Crocosmia* 'Lucifer' and *Hemerocallis*. This is a similar concept to the Long Island *Stipa* meadow, but with a wider selection of plants that will remain attractive into winter.

←

So far we have seen primarily flat or sloping sites where plants alone have provided gradations of height, mostly noticeable from late spring onwards. This part of the Clos du Coudray garden in Normandy, designed by Jean le Bret, was dug out of surrounding farmland to make a sunken pathway that meanders through raised, sloping beds planted with a variety of perennials and grasses. On this early autumn day drifts of *Stipa tenuissima* (foreground), *Gaura lindheimeri* (right), *Molinia caerulea* 'Variegata' with autumnal tinges (centre near pathway) and the hazy *Stipa gigantea* in the distance contrast with the still-green foliage of *Miscanthus*. Foliage is the mainstay of this garden, interrupted by seasonal splashes of colour.

→

This new garden, designed and planted by passionate gardeners Keith and Roz Wiley in Devon, England, is photographed only three years after planting, displaying an eclectic and exciting mix of woody and herbaceous plants. Keith raised his beds not only to add drama to the landscape, but also to create different environments to suit his wide choice of plants. Thus south-, north-, east- and west-facing slopes from top to bottom create a range of conditions not otherwise available together on a single site. Close planting has already lent a maturing look to this colourful garden, as well as helping to keep weeds at bay.

→

You wouldn't have guessed that Hurricane Isabel had smashed up much of plantswoman Pamela Harper's Virginia garden four years before this photograph was taken. This is a generously sized suburban garden with a difference: an amazing collection of woody and perennial plants, well-designed and effectively combined. A paved stone pathway takes an informal and meandering course, a fastigiate yew a distant focal point. On a warm day in spring, new fresh green growth and foliage allow a small group of early-flowering *Hemerocallis dumortieri* to shine in front of the purple foliage and white flowers of *Physocarpus opulifolius* 'Diabolo'.

→

Some gardens can be taken in with one glance, but Tim and Isabella Vaughan's garden in Brittany, France needs time for the visitor to absorb its many levels and layers of planting: part control and part exuberant freedom. On a wet day in early autumn this garden retains foliage and flower colour, with yellow *Hakonechloa* and *Kniphofia* in the foreground around the sunken garden and a vibrant group of scarlet, purple-leaved dahlias in the background. Mounds of regularly pruned evergreen shrubs add subdued colour, create individual controlled forms and provide some winter interest. The blue-flowered plant cascading over the wall in the foreground is the tender *Convolvulus sabatius*.

← Creating year-round interest can be quite simple if you rely on foliage. The woody shrub *Cornus alba* 'Aurea' has golden leaves in summer, good autumn colour and deep red stems in winter, while the narrowly columnar *Taxus baccata* 'Fastigiata' changes little through the seasons. In the Summer Garden at Bressingham, [→] I've tried to create a breaking wave with the Japanese hakone grass, *Hakonechloa macra*, green in summer, tawny then beige through much of winter. This is 'breaking' over the black-leaved sea of *Ophiopogon planiscapus* 'Nigrescens', with tiny lilac-mauve flowers in summer, edged with frost in winter.

↙ A 'dry garden' is a term relative to where you live as well as to your soil conditions. Few climates are more demanding than in the region near Melbourne, Australia, with prolonged summer temperatures of 40°C (104°F) and above, and to create such a garden needs attention to design along with a careful selection of drought- and heat-resistant plants (plus hard work). This beautiful garden at Lambley Nursery in Acton, Victoria belongs to nurseryman and gardener David Glenn and renowned Australian artist Criss Canning who both contributed to its design through their artistry and plantsmanship. A background hedge and grey-leaved olive trees draw the eye across a mixed planting showing colour and form, the rounded heads of *Sedum* 'Matrona' in the foreground contrasting with spiked leaves of *Yucca gloriosa*.

→

Can a sustainable, environmentally friendly garden also be attractive year-round, and what role can perennials and grasses play? Photographer, designer of ecological landscapes and authority on grasses Rick Darke experiments with his own rural woodland edge Pennsylvania garden. Although he has a rich selection of eastern United States natives to call upon, he is not averse to fitting in similar-climate plants from Asia, or other countries. His main design ethic is that no supplemental watering should be required, no chemical

pest or weed control practised and plants should fit in naturally with the surrounding countryside.

Mostly textured foliage in shades of green provides a cool environment in spring and on hot summer days, the greatest colour arriving with autumn as shown here with mounds of drought-resistant *Aster oblongifolius*, the aromatic aster, flowing cascading grasses and russet autumn leaves. In the future, more and more gardeners may be moving in this environmentally friendly direction.

→

What of the small garden? A back garden has the privacy and size to be used as a family playground and relaxation area, and once the children have grown it could become more design- and plant-orientated. The front garden is seen daily, even if not used, and plants can bring it alive. In this 6 × 6-m (20 × 20-ft.) front garden in Roydon, England, perennials, grasses and a few woody plants brighten what was previously a grass lawn. The smaller the garden, the more important it is to select plants for continuity of colour. Caring for these plants will take no more time than mowing the lawn, but is certainly more therapeutic and environmentally friendly.

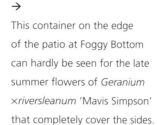

← Summer sunlight filters through the reddening leaves of *Imperata cylindrica* 'Rubra'.

→ This container on the edge of the patio at Foggy Bottom can hardly be seen for the late summer flowers of *Geranium ×riversleanum* 'Mavis Simpson' that completely cover the sides.

A Moveable Feast: Perennials and Ornamental Grasses in Containers

When it comes to growing plants in pots and containers, conifers, shrubs and annuals, particularly the latter, have long been favourites for providing colour and interest, especially in small gardens where there is a shortage of space. But there are also many perennials and ornamental grasses that should be more widely used.

Ideally you should choose a plant that will look good in a container for weeks, maybe months, which limits the selection. It is probably not advisable to use plants that grow too rapidly or need staking either.

Over years of experimenting with many perennials and ornamental grasses in patio containers, I've observed that they fall into three main categories. First are those that have compact habits, and whose foliage and flower are attractive over a long season: *Brunnera macrophylla* 'Jack Frost', *Campanula poscharskyana* 'Blue Waterfall' and *Hosta* 'Halcyon' are examples. (If you can keep the slugs at bay, hostas are ideal for growing in containers, particularly for shady or semi-shady positions, though any of these plants if left outside will die down in winter.) Slightly less compact, but striking and useful, are long-flowering hardy geraniums including *G.* 'Rozanne' and *Geranium ×riversleanum* 'Mavis

Simpson'. Second are evergreens used on their own or in conjunction with other plants such as *Ophiopogon planiscapus* 'Nigrescens', *Acorus gramineus* 'Ogon', *Bergenia* 'Bressingham Ruby' and *Carex*. Finally there are the more architectural plants; in this third category I would include the indispensable *Hakonechloa macra* 'Alboaurea' plus other hakone grasses, *Miscanthus sinensis* 'Gold Bar', *Chionochloa rubra* and *Molinia caerulea* 'Variegata'. Kniphofias and agapanthus are striking too, but they have long summer periods when they lack interest.

Perennials and grasses should be grown in a reasonably open compost, ideally with sufficient fertilizer to last a full growing season. For the following years add a slow-release granular fertilizer to cover each season unless you have a drip feed fertilizing system. Getting any well-established plant out of some containers can be a problem. Lining with polythene prior to potting may help, as perennials and grasses will need dividing and re-potting every few years. Containers are in theory a moveable commodity, but the larger they get the more difficult they become. We use a sack barrow, which helps, but you need two people to help manoeuvre your containers to a new position. As ever, plants in containers need watering—and while they should not be too wet, perennials and grasses should never be allowed to dry out in the summer.

↑

Cornus sanguinea 'Midwinter Fire' makes a colourful display in a container on its own in winter, but underplanting with *Ophiopogon planiscapus* 'Nigrescens' and *Galanthus nivalis* 'S. Arnott' completes the picture, almost creating a stand-alone winter garden.

↓

If you can keep the slugs away, hostas are perfect for patio containers. The architectural form of *Hosta* 'Sagae' adds to its brightly variegated leaves in late spring.

↑

By early midsummer when *Campanula poscharskyana* is in flower, the brilliant golden-variegated *Hakonechloa macra* 'Alboaurea' is already the star of the show in a container.

↓

For a semi-shady spot, the combination of *Brunnera macrophylla* 'Jack Frost' tumbling over the black leaves of *Ophiopogon planiscapus* 'Nigrescens', enhanced by a black pot, makes for a long-interest container of foliage perennials, seen here in late summer.

TAKE TWELVE PLANTS:
A Key to Successful Gardening

In summer, *M. s.* 'Morning Light' adds a light touch of vertical foliage to *Geranium* 'Rozanne' in the foreground, and contrasts with the rich green specimen conifer *Thuja occidentalis*

'Smaragd' behind, in the zu Jeddeloh garden I designed in Germany. *Agastache* 'Blue Fortune' and *Crocosmia* 'Lucifer' light up the background.

For many years, one of my greatest ambitions been to get more people switched on to gardening. To me, the benefits of gardening are self-evident: whatever the size of a residence, plants can beautify it—from the smallest patio, terrace or window box to a suburban or larger country garden and landscape. Gardening allows us to be creative with living things and to better understand nature, the weather and our surroundings. In our often time-pressed lives, gardening allows us moments to relax and become absorbed in a therapeutic pastime. And of course, on the practical side, a well-tended garden can add value to a property.

Realistically, though, work, family and social obligations sometimes leave little time or inclination for gardening, particularly for those younger than 45 or so. To others it seems too complicated, difficult to know where to start or just too much work. New or even relatively experienced gardeners can be confused by the massive choice of ornamental plants available, and to discern which might be best for their gardens may seem daunting. For instance, at Bressingham, we have around 8,000 species and cultivars of plants on display: great to visit, enjoy and perhaps draw inspiration from, but sometimes our visitors find the sheer quantity of plants available to be overwhelming and bewildering—when in truth only a fraction of these plants may be suitable for their garden conditions or even gardenworthy.

Over the years, I have come to understand that in the garden less can often be more. While planting up Foggy Bottom and other gardens at Bressingham, developing small front gardens using primarily perennials and grasses in England and North America, and then designing larger demonstration and educational gardens in Germany and the United States, I have come to rely on a core of relatively few but very special plants. While not perfect for every situation (and hardly any plants are), between them these plants can provide year-round interest, often in the form of spectacular flower and foliage that changes with the seasons. They can be used in combination with each other, or with many other plants, including shrubs. I have gradually narrowed this list down to twelve perennials and ornamental grasses.

Why so few? Reducing the focus to twelve tried-and-tested plants allows us to study and learn about a small group, each capable of creating drama in almost any garden, especially when enhanced by clever plant combination and good design. They are useful in large groups as well as smaller combinations. With the focus on just twelve plants, not only can we manage to remember the plants' names (some are quite difficult!) but we can also begin to observe and learn how each changes through the seasons, and in turn how we can live with them—following their natural progression, alone and with other plants, from growth surge in spring, through glory in summer, to maturity in autumn and then dormancy or flower in winter, depending on where you garden. Watch how they are affected by the wind and the rain, or even the heat and drought, the autumn mist or winter frost, and enjoy the low winter light as it highlights the shrubs, grasses or perennials.

In this chapter and in other sections of this book you will see these twelve selected perennials and grasses in different situations and at different times of the year, along with some simple yet effective ideas for developing your own year-round garden with key long-interest plants. They can be used with woody shrubs or conifers, or with other plants of your choice. As with any new subject it might be helpful to grow your knowledge from small beginnings, perhaps starting with a small area of your garden. More complete descriptions, including dimensions and cultural details, can be found in the Directory.

Using these twelve plants it is surprisingly simple to create attractive long-term plant combinations in any size of garden. For instance, in sun where not too dry consider using *Miscanthus sinensis* 'Morning Light' as your specimen plant. In a small garden, surround the miscanthus with one specimen each of *Geranium* 'Rozanne', *Crocosmia* 'Lucifer', *Actaea simplex* 'Brunette' (on the shadier side), *Sedum* 'Matrona' and *Rudbeckia fulgida* var. *sullivantii* 'Goldsturm', planting at least 60 cm (2 ft.) apart.

In larger areas, try three to five miscanthus planted in a semi-circle or staggered at least 180–240 cm (6–8 ft.) apart and use groups of varying numbers of the other five cultivars in between. These will make a spectacular show from midsummer into winter.

For a lower-growing display with year-round interest for sun or half shade depending on climate, combine varying numbers of *Bergenia* 'Bressingham Ruby', *Hakonechloa macra* 'Alboaurea', *Brunnera macrophylla* 'Jack Frost', *Ophiopogon planiscapus* 'Nigrescens', *Hosta* 'Francee' and *Helleborus* ×*hybridus*. Imagine a 'river' of the ophiopogon or brunnera flowering through a shady, not-too-dry area flanked by informal drifts of some of the other varieties, adding a generous sprinkle of snowdrops and other small bulbs in winter. Don't forget that many will work well in containers and with other plants in your garden to add drama and excitement. Less, in this case, can indeed be more.

1

Ophiopogon planiscapus 'Nigrescens'

black mondo grass

At a glance

Once established, black mondo grass makes a year-round carpet of jet black leaves, good in shade where not too dry, and excellent in a container. It has a multitude of uses—as ground cover beneath shrubs or trees, or as a pathway edging—and will associate well with *Brunnera macrophylla* 'Jack Frost', *Hosta* 'Francee' and *Hakonechloa macra* 'Alboaurea'.

Period of interest

throughout the year

↖

In summer, in the shade of *Cornus sanguinea* 'Midwinter Fire', the ophiopogon makes little impact. But when leaves drop on the dogwood to reveal fiery winter stems, the black mondo grass adds a dramatic contrast, softened here in late winter by cheerful snowdrops.·

↑

Ophiopogon planiscapus 'Nigrescens' has small but attractive lilac purple flowers in summer followed by shiny black fruits in autumn and winter. Both leaves and flowers stand out in this rusty metal patio container, behind which is the side of another similar but taller pot.

↑

Helleborus hybrids with painted petals are very much a part of this small early spring grouping, timed to coincide with snowdrops (*Galanthus nivalis*) and aconites (*Eranthis hyemalis*) in the Royal Horticultural Society's Gardens at Wisley. When the surrounding bulbs die back in summer, the foliage of the *Helleborus* will cover the ground for the rest of the year. Blue-flowered bulbs such as *Scilla sibirica* and *Chionodoxa lucillae* can also create a striking carpet beneath *Helleborus* flowers.

↑

The main parent of the *Helleborus* ×*hybridus* group is *H. orientalis*, the Lenten rose, which this plant closely resembles, the pendulous maroon flowers and yellow stamens making a striking contrast to late winter snow. In both pictures, last year's foliage has been cut away to highlight the flowers.

↑

Plant breeders have been busy in England, Germany and North America in recent years, producing an amazing array of colours and forms of *Helleborus hybridus*. One of the most prolific has been Ashwood Nurseries in England. This black-petalled selection is one of the *H.* ×*h.* Ashwood Garden hybrids which, like most of these hybrids, will last for years once planted.

2 *Helleborus* ×*hybridus*

hellebore

At a glance

These superb easy-growing plants come in many colours, growing well in sun or shade in cool climates and preferring some shade in hotter regions. They do well in most soils except badly drained. Flowers emerge in late winter and early spring; they make their best display when the previous year's foliage is cut away at ground level before flowering. With good green foliage, they make excellent ground cover in summer.

Period of interest

throughout the year

←

In late winter the morning sun catches the broad reddish purple leaves of Bergenia 'Bressingham Ruby', growing beneath clumps of the impressive New Zealand sedge *Chionochloa rubra*. This is a reasonably moist position, but *Bergenia* 'Bressingham Ruby' will take quite dry conditions too; in fact, this can even make the colour more pronounced.

3 *Bergenia* 'Bressingham Ruby'

bergenia, pigsqueak, elephant's ears

At a glance

There are many different species and cultivars of *Bergenia* that are useful for ground cover in sun or part shade, but few are as outstanding as 'Bressingham Ruby', with bright green heart-shaped summer leaves that turn to deep ruby red with purple undersides in winter. Of easy cultivation, the best colour will come from those planted in a sunny situation. Deep rose pink flowers are an added bonus in spring.

Period of interest
throughout the year

↑
New bright green leaves emerge in spring to coincide with the striking flowers of *Bergenia* 'Bressingham Ruby'. At any time (and particularly in spring), shabby, blackened or dying leaves should be removed. The remainder will be green all summer.

↑
Another transformation is about to occur in autumn, the deepening green leaves of *Bergenia* 'Bressingham Ruby' making a great contrast to the long-lasting golden autumn foliage of *Cornus sanguinea* 'Midwinter Fire'. As leaves and temperature drop, the *Bergenia* foliage turns to deep ruby—to enjoy throughout winter, except when covered by snow.

4 *Brunnera macrophylla* 'Jack Frost'

heartleaf brunnera, Siberian bugloss

At a glance

One of the most attractive and useful foliage and flowering perennials, it has few faults, growing easily in sun or shade where not too dry. Early forget-me-not spring flowers are followed by broad heart-shaped silvery leaves edged and finely veined with green. Cutting back leaves and watering in late summer will renew with bright new foliage. Many combinations are possible; for instance, use between shrubs as ground cover.

Period of interest

spring to late autumn

↖

A mass of pale blue forget-me-not flowers in spring contrast with a few heads of *Tulipa* 'Queen of the Night' and a purple-leaved Japanese maple behind. When flowering has finished, cut back stems and older leaves, leaving new foliage to develop.

↑

The marbled silvery surface of the summer foliage of *B. m.* 'Jack Frost' is a wonder of nature, although this plant arose not as a chance seedling but as a mutation in the micropropagation laboratory at Walters Gardens in Michigan. All cultivars of *B. m.* seed freely, but will most likely be different from the parent.

5 Hosta 'Francee'

plantain lily

At a glance

When it comes to deciding which hostas to grow, foliage and flower should be considered, as well as their form and vigour, and how well they combine with other plants. *Hosta* 'Francee' was introduced in 1986 and is still considered one of the best, now classic, variegated hostas to enjoy from the first buds in spring until autumn. Best in part shade, it mixes well with woodland plants and in perennial beds. The flowers are excellent, and despite being prone to slugs and snails it is easy, long-lived and of tremendous value in the garden.

Period of interest

spring to autumn

↑

The maturing, now-spreading glossy foliage of *Hosta* 'Francee' is still holding up well in mid to late summer next to the evergreen fern *Dryopteris*

erythrosaura. You can usually rely on this cultivar to produce a good display of lily-like lavender flowers each year plus golden leaves in autumn.

←

Hostas are slow to start new growth in spring, but given warm weather the pointed shoots break through the surface of the soil and rapidly begin to unfurl. At this stage, the erect young leaves are at their brightest: finely ribbed and edged with creamy white, catching the early morning sun.

6 *Geranium* 'Rozanne'

hardy geranium, cranesbill

At a glance
When this plant was first introduced in 2000, I had no hesitation in naming it "the hardy geranium of the new millennium", having grown it for six years just 3 m (10 ft.) from our house where we could enjoy it every day it was in bloom. Hardy, long-lived, amazingly long-flowering and easy to grow, it is a perennial that every garden should have. I have grown *Geranium* 'Rozanne' in the garden (you just might see a few more pictures of it elsewhere in the book), in a container, hanging basket and window box—a truly versatile plant. A decade on, gardeners, nursery growers and designers across the world are singing the praises of 'Rozanne': need I say more? And of course one can think of a multitude of associations for it, including as a 'river'.

Period of interest
early summer to late autumn

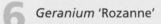

↖
Geranium 'Rozanne' is a chance hybrid between the early-flowering *G. himalayense* and later-blooming *G. wallichianum* 'Buxton's Variety' which arose in the Somerset, England garden of Donald and Rozanne Waterer. Here some flowers have strayed into *Sedum* 'Matrona' in late summer.

↑
'Rozanne' in close-up, splashed with droplets of a summer shower.

→
Geranium 'Rozanne' is a vigorous free-flowering perennial, seen here making a colourful and dramatic combination in the Summer Garden at Bressingham with *Crocosmia* 'Lucifer', always the first crocosmia to flower.

←

The mid spring foliage of *Actaea simplex* 'Brunette' with black arching stems and divided black purple leaves makes a striking centrepiece in Foggy Bottom to *Geranium himalayense* in the foreground, *Hosta* 'Krossa Regal', *Symphytum uplandicum* 'Variegatum' and the pink bottlebrush heads of *Persicaria bistorta* 'Superbum' behind.

↓

Late summer foliage is taking a reddish, faded tinge in this open position in the Dell Garden at Bressingham as a succession of flowerheads emerge, black in bud opening to pinkish white and delightfully fragrant.

7 *Actaea simplex* 'Brunette'

bugbane

At a glance

Far more adaptable than most gardeners realize, *A. s.* 'Brunette' (formerly listed as *Cimicifuga simplex* 'Brunette') is a classy plant with large leaves of rich purple-black, which in reasonably shady positions hold their colour into autumn. They do best where conditions are not too dry. In early autumn, tall purple spikes are topped by poker heads of delicate white, pink-tinged, fragrant flowers that continue for weeks, with attractive seedheads soon to follow. Associate it with *Brunnera macrophylla* 'Jack Frost', *Geranium* 'Rozanne' or *Hakonechloa macra* 'Alboaurea' to name but a few.

Period of interest
spring to winter

↑

In late summer and autumn, wispy flowers show up in the foliage of *Hakonechloa macra* 'Alboaurea'. Here on an autumn day in Foggy Bottom it is making good ground cover beneath a pine tree, surrounded by the lower-growing *Ophiopogon planiscapus* 'Nigrescens' and the autumn foliage of *Hosta* 'Krossa Regal'. The group beneath *Tsuga canadensis* 'Bennett' is *Hakonechloa macra* 'Allgold'.

↑

As winter comes, the leaves of *H. m.* 'Alboaurea' die but remain on the plant, turning to gold then beige, and here in midwinter making an almost stronger contrast to *Ophiopogon* than in summer. The fern is *Polystichum setiferum* (Divisilobum Group) 'Divisilobum Densum'.

↓

A mature clump of *Hakonechloa macra* 'Alboaurea' makes a graceful mound of overlapping leaves beside a pathway on a summer morning at the New York Botanical Garden. The foliage is so light that even a breeze will ruffle the leaves.

8 *Hakonechloa macra* 'Alboaurea'

golden variegated hakone grass

At a glance

What a beautiful and spectacular plant this can be. With a long period of interest and many uses in the garden, it is excellent in a container on a terrace or patio. From bright yellow mid spring shoots to summer and autumn mounds of gold and green with gracefully overlapping foliage, this grass still remains attractive into winter. Grow in sun or part shade where not too dry. Try it with *Ophiopogon planiscapus* 'Nigrescens', *Brunnera macrophylla* 'Jack Frost', *Bergenia* 'Bressingham Ruby', *Geranium* 'Rozanne' and blue-leaved hostas such as *H.* 'Halcyon'.

Period of interest
spring to midwinter

9 *Crocosmia* 'Lucifer'

crocosmia, montbretia

At a glance

Introduced in England in 1966 along with several other gardenworthy hybrids, the fiery C. 'Lucifer' has for many years been the most widely grown and popular cultivar of these South African natives. (They are actually corms, similar to bulbs.) Tough and vigorous but not invasive, C. 'Lucifer' is also attractive for its bright green sword-like leaves before spectacular vermillion-crimson flowers open in midsummer. The flowers are excellent for cutting, as are later seedheads. Associate in perennial and grass borders, in front of purple shrubs or blue-leaved conifers.

Period of interest

early to late summer and autumn

↖
Crocosmia 'Lucifer' is as exotic in close-up as in the garden. Arching flowers are held on black stems opening from the bottom to top—an excellent cut flower.

↑
The green sword-like leaves and glowing vermillion flowers of *Crocosmia* 'Lucifer' make a startling contrast with a blue fir, *Abies lasiocarpa* var. *arizonica* 'Compacta', at Foggy Bottom.

↑

Small droplets of morning dew on the lightly variegated foliage of *Miscanthus sinensis* 'Morning Light' enhance its arching, elegant appearance in the Summer Garden at Bressingham in late summer.

↓

In late winter in Foggy Bottom after frost and snow, the foliage of *Miscanthus sinensis* 'Morning Light' is still enjoyed—for its graceful presence, its tawny beige colour next to a golden-leaved conifer, the winter light that filters through it, and the way it moves in the wind.

10 *Miscanthus sinensis* 'Morning Light'

silver grass

At a glance

If you had to choose one miscanthus to use in your garden—to grow well, have good summer-long foliage and hold up nicely in winter—you could not choose anything better than *M. s.* 'Morning Light'. With narrow white-striped leaves, upright but not rigid structure and the ability to act as a specimen or blend in with perennials in a bed or border, *M. s.* 'Morning Light' is the perfect plant. Growing to 120–150 cm (4–5 ft.) in most situations, it is suitable for most gardens. Like many non-evergreen grasses that gradually die back in late autumn, the foliage still offers a long period of interest during winter.

Period of interest

early summer to late winter

11 *Sedum* 'Matrona'

sedum, stonecrop

At a glance
To be selected for its versatility, adaptability and long period of interest each plant in this chapter must be outstanding, and *Sedum* 'Matrona' holds to that standard. Not only is it very hardy and reliable but it also withstands heat and drought, and from early succulent grey-green foliage in spring to reddening stems and rose-pink flowers in late summer *S.* 'Matrona' gives excellent value. The autumn and winter seedheads are a bonus until spring growth begins again. Use with *Geranium* 'Rozanne', *Miscanthus sinensis* 'Morning Light', *Panicum virgatum* 'Northwind' and many other perennials and grasses.

Period of interest
throughout most of the year

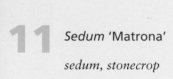

A closer look at *Sedum* 'Matrona' reveals its crimson-purple stems and succulent leaves, highlighted in a sunny, dry position in front of *Helenium* 'Pipsqueak'. Watching this and other perennials develop through a long season from spring to winter shows what a living entity gardening is.

Clusters of flower buds held on purple-red branched stems give *Sedum* 'Matrona' a distinctive appearance in the foreground of this association of perennials and grasses in the Summer Garden at Bressingham. Its deeper tones add a welcome contrast to the bright yellow *Crocosmia* ×*crocosmiiflora* 'Canary Bird' and magenta flowers of *Geranium* 'Patricia' through which the brightly striped vertical leaves of *Miscanthus sinensis* 'Variegatus' emerge.

→
How often do we examine our garden flowers in true close-up, appreciating their elegance and beauty of form and dramatic contrasts of colour? A sense of wonder, too, might cross the mind upon looking closely at a single flower of *Rudbeckia fulgida* var. *sullivantii* 'Goldsturm'.

↘
This self-sown clump of *R. f.* var. *s.* 'Goldsturm' could not have arisen in a better place in Foggy Bottom. Three or four years later it is making a bold late summer display in front of a blue spruce, *Picea pungens* 'Globosa', and behind the (by now rather unkempt) inflorescences of *Stipa tenuissima*. Even when flowers have finished, the seedheads remain attractive in winter.

12 *Rudbeckia fulgida* var. *sullivantii* 'Goldsturm'

orange coneflower, black-eyed susan

At a glance
The taxonomists have given us a real mouthful with the extended name of this popular perennial, but *Rudbeckia* 'Goldsturm' will do for most of us—and most expert and experienced gardeners would put *Rudbeckia f.* var. *s.* 'Goldsturm' among their top ten perennials. To me, it is not only a joyous and cheery plant but also an easy and reliable grower that will give pleasure for many years. From mats of glossy deep green leaves, closed buds on slender stems erupt in a mass of bloom for weeks in late summer and early autumn, given an open position where not too dry. Good partners include *Geranium* 'Rozanne', *Stipa tenuissima*, *Aster* ×*frikartii* 'Monch' and *Miscanthus sinensis* 'Morning Light'.

Period of interest
midsummer to winter

CHOOSING PERENNIALS
AND GRASSES

←

Low, medium and tall perennials and grasses are shown in late summer, at their peak of annual growth in Foggy Bottom. The miniature black-eyed susan *Rudbeckia fulgida* VIETTE'S LITTLE SUZY 'Blovi' is in the foreground, above it to the left *Miscanthus sinensis* 'Morning Light'. *Aster laterifolius* 'Prince' with deep purple foliage is sandwiched between *R. f.* VIETTE'S LITTLE SUZY 'Blovi' and *R. f.* var. *sullivantii* 'Goldsturm', and the two most imposing clumps of *Eupatorium maculatum* 'Gateway' give height and drama to the planting of mostly summer-flowering perennials.

So many garden plants are available today that choosing the best for your garden can be overwhelming. Among all of the genera, species and cultivars, there are probably at least 50,000 selections of perennials and ornamental grasses, wild and cultivated across the temperate regions of the world. From the lowly *Lamium maculatum* or *Ajuga reptans* that grow to 15 cm (6 in.) to the towering *Eupatorium maculatum* 'Gateway' and *Rudbeckia laciniata* 'Herbstsonne', and several cultivars of *Miscanthus sinensis*, which in reasonably moist conditions will reach 2.4 m (8 ft.) in one season, there are perennials and grasses to fit any size of garden or landscape. From waterside or bog plants such as *Caltha*, *Lythrum* and *Ligularia* to those loving hot dry conditions such as *Acanthus*, *Eryngium*, *Gaura* and *Stokesia*, there are innumerable choices in between.

In the *Plant Finder*, published annually by the Royal Horticultural Society for gardeners in Britain, between 1992 and 2009 the number of *Phlox paniculata* cultivars increased from 83 to 244. Although much breeding work has been undertaken with this plant (see page 61), *P. paniculata* isn't an anomaly: the number of *Pulmonaria* species and cultivars rose from 54 to 131, those of *Heuchera* grew from 50 to 185 and hardy *Geranium* species and cultivars rose from 255 to a staggering 733 (an exceptional, nearly threefold increase; they self-hybridize readily, and they have been very fashionable). Ornamental grasses became increasingly popular in the mid 1980s; *Pennisetum* rose from nine to 38 and, most dramatically, *Miscanthus* from 37 species and cultivars to 112.

For some—plant-collectors, perhaps, or those with very large gardens—this dizzying choice may a benefit, and undoubtedly some excellent and much-improved cultivars have come to the fore. Yet for most gardeners such proliferation will be bewildering. Even those in the horticultural industry, from propagators to landscape designers, struggle to keep abreast of the growth of new cultivars and select the best. While many of the new cultivars have been bred for specific purposes such as a more compact habit, longer flowering period or resistance to mildew or disease, many more of the plants promoted and displayed on garden centre benches have come onto the market largely untested and untrialled in gardens and landscapes; it is left up to the gardener to do the trialling, often with poor results.

Tips for Selecting Plants

While glossy close-up photographs of flowers in gardening books, magazines and catalogues may look beautiful, you need more information in order judge their garden worthiness—and although "plant in sun, give good drainage" might be the basic cultural information on a plant's label, longer-term success rests on finding out more about your plants' preferences.

There is no such thing as a perfect plant, but some come much closer than others. In order to make the best choice you should ideally be considering (in no order of importance): preference, if any, for acid or alkaline (limey) soils, dislike of winter wet or summer drought, flowering period, how many weeks or months it remains attractive in flower, its foliage or seedheads, whether it is a robust or

The purple foliage of *Physocarpus opulifolius* 'Diabolo' acts as a strong background contrast to the already vivid green sword-like foliage and brilliant vermillion flowers of *Crocosmia* 'Lucifer' in this midsummer combination in Foggy Bottom. Using such striking foliage can make for more dramatic combinations in the garden.

believe that some 'icons' of the perennial world fail to give sufficient value. Judged on their spectacular beauty at the height of flowering, for instance, it would be difficult to fault most cultivars of *Iris germanica*—but judge them on longevity of performance and contribution to the garden for the following 11 months and they fail miserably. Hit a warm spell when your *Paeonia lactiflora* varieties come into flower and, beautiful as they are, they'll be gone in a flash. A reliable and reasonably long-flowering performance coupled with the ability to blend naturally with other plants is ideal (and key to my selection process).

Plan for Foliage Through the Seasons

To extend colour and interest, to create drama and contrast, to produce coolness and clarity—plants grown primarily for their foliage are vital to the gardener. Shades of green, gold or yellow, purple, silver or variegated can be found in trees, shrubs or conifers. Overuse of the brighter colours may be distracting or dazzling, particularly when similar foliage colours of perennials are added (plus flower colours). Being selective in foliage colour use and combination can add dramatic touches. Purple-leaved shrubs such as *Cotinus coggygria* 'Royal Purple', *Physocarpus opulifolius* 'Diabolo' or *Cercis canadensis* 'Forest Pansy' can make a dramatic background contrast to both the bright green strap-like foliage and the brilliant vermillion flame flowers of *Crocosmia* 'Lucifer'. In recent years the proliferation of hostas, heucheras and tiarellas has given us some wonderful foliage plants, while ornamental grasses such as *Festuca glauca*, *Hakonechloa macra* and its cultivars, *Ophiopogon planiscapus* 'Nigrescens' with

weak grower or has an invasive habit, whether it is particularly susceptible to any pest or disease and of course whether in your climate or region it is a truly hardy plant, if that is important to you.

Create a Festival of Flowers

Perennial species and cultivars are mostly valued for adding flower colour to the garden from spring until autumn—traditionally woodland species and wildflowers in spring, classic perennials such as irises, peonies, hemerocallis and *Phlox paniculata* in summer, and asters leavened by sedums, rudbeckias and heliopsis in autumn.

Today we have more colourful perennials to choose from than ever before. Having long considered the relative merit of plants in the year-round garden, I personally

↓

Astilbes are showy plants for
moist conditions and need shade
in hotter climates. The most
tolerant group for drier soils
are the *A. Chinensis* Group of
species and cultivars such as *A. c.*
'Visions' shown here in summer.

its year-round black leaves, and many others mentioned in the Directory are great options.

Avoid Square Pegs in Round Holes

Plants are, of course, more likely to succeed when provided with conditions that suit them. Take those wonderful, very cold-hardy astilbes, for instance, with their feathery plumes of vibrant colours. They do well in full sun with good summer moisture in the cooler northern temperate zones, northern England and Scotland and Nova Scotia to Quebec, flowering for a few weeks. Proceeding further south, with hotter summers they will need more shade and moisture, will flower for a much shorter period and if they get dry, foliage will quickly crisp and scorch. Unless conditions are favourable, using plants that need a lot of work or maintenance to succeed are best avoided, unless you really want a challenge.

Beware of Thugs (or Contain Them)

Whether a plant already prone to invasiveness will become a nuisance depends largely on climate and soil conditions; its invasiveness can vary widely from one area to another. The pungent but colourful summer foliage of the Japanese perennial *Houttuynia cordata* 'Chameleon' makes quite an impact with its brilliant orange, red and yellow leaves. Give it a moist free running soil in the warm summers of most of North America and it will quickly spread into every nook and cranny, yet in cooler British summers in average soils it makes a spreading but hardly invasive clump. Most of us know ground elder, *Aegopodium podogaria*, as a weed with spreading white

roots and bright green leaves. We would not touch it with a bargepole, but the variegated form *A. p.* 'Variegata', undeniably attractive as a shade plant, can be equally weedy and invasive. Ideally, both *A. p.* 'Variegata' and

↓

The invasive *Houttuynia cordata* 'Chameleon' is banned from sale in some countries, and is best not planted in any garden. Yet when held captive in a patio container, it makes an attractive foliage plant.

Houttuynia cordata 'Chameleon', being attractive foliage plants, should always kept 'captive' and grown only in pots or containers.

The Importance of Origins

To predict how a plant might perform it is always useful to investigate its origins, especially the conditions under which it grows in its native land and habitat, as this may give a clue about its ability to thrive in your garden. For instance, plants grown around the Mediterranean Sea which divides Europe from Africa often do well in the mediterranean climates of coastal California and parts of Australia and New Zealand, and vice versa. Mid to northern Japan and parts of China have similar climates to the eastern and midwestern United States, with hot humid summers and warm ripening autumns—something we seldom experience in Britain and northern Europe, although to an extent this may eventually change due to global warming.

Knowing that the false indigo, *Baptisia australis* (the species name meaning 'southern', not 'originating from Australia'!), is native to the midwestern United States, from the western Appalachian Mountains in the east, west across to the plains of Kansas, south to Georgia and across to Texas, tells you it must tolerate summer heat and be winter hardy. More research will reveal that it grows in the wild in open woods, sandy flood plains and river banks, informing you that it needs an open situation, may tolerate shade and prefers some moisture, at least in spring.

→

Not all of the older *Phlox paniculata* cultivars were bred in Europe. Enjoying a renewed popularity is *P. p.* 'Katherine', with white-centred petals suffusing into lilac-blue edges. You can only imagine the perfume. *P. p.* 'Katherine' was raised around 1920 at the then-famous nursery of Martin Viette near New York City. It is mildew resistant and grows to 90 cm (3 ft.).

Garden Perennials in Perspective

The practice of importing perennials to European gardens has its main roots in the 17th century, when many European countries began to push out their boundaries to create overseas dominions. A flood of 'novelty' plants were brought back from faraway places to adorn the garden of landowners with great estates, wealth and power—yet it was exotic trees and shrubs, not lowly grasses and perennials, that were considered most desirable. Later, during the Victorian era, labour-intensive annual bedding was all the rage. It was not until the late 19th century that perennials really came into favour, with influential British gardeners William Robinson and Gertrude Jekyll popularizing their use. Interest grew in other European countries, too, with the artistic mixture of perennials with other plants immortalized in Monet's garden in Giverny a famous case in point.

In the early years of perennial selection, plants were largely introduced and bred by amateur gardeners and professional nurserymen across Europe who imported species from Japan, China, South Africa, South America and above all North America. In the United States, following westward expansion, plant-hunters—mainly British, but some American—were collecting and funnelling a wide range of plant species from their native North America to Europe, including perennials from the genera *Dicentra*, *Echinacea*, *Heuchera*, *Helenium*, *Monarda*, *Aster* and *Phlox*.

Phlox paniculata (border phlox), for instance, originated in the United States, from New York, west across Ohio to Kansas and south to Arkansas and northern Georgia. Probably first collected in 1743 by the well-known American plant-hunter John Bartrum, the plants were sent overseas where the species was to undergo extensive breeding work in England (beginning in 1824 by G. Wheeler of Warminster, Wiltshire), Germany, the Netherlands and France. From 1839, the Frenchman M. Lierval brought out more selections, and it was not long before border phlox cultivars, improving in flower colour, panicle size and constitution, became fashionable and much sought after by gardeners in Europe—and in time, rather ironically, they were also exported back to the increasingly wealthy citizens of the United States.

It is curious how gardeners often value plants from 'exotic' places above their own. Until well into the 20th century, North American gardeners had looked to Europe, and particularly English-speaking Britain, for their garden inspiration, often believing British plants to be more highly bred or 'civilized'. It is only in recent years that countries have become more aware of, and prepared to consider or even demand, their own natives. Now, once again in Europe and North America, native species and cultivars are reaching unprecedented levels of popularity.

Sun-loving *Eryngium bourgatii* growing at altitude among rocks in the San Gloria Picos mountains in northern Spain. Very hardy in its natural habitat, it is more likely to be short lived in gardens due to wet winter soils and poor drainage.

→

Helenium bigelovii, one of the parents of most of our garden heleniums, flowering in late summer by a fast-flowing stream in King's Canyon National Park in California.

Coming from another angle, a North American native and one of the most popular perennials with a mouthful of a name, *Rudbeckia fulgida* var. *sullivantii* 'Goldsturm', was mostly grown in Britain as a sun lover, requiring a warm, sunny position. By chance, when a large group of the plants was under water in our Foggy Bottom garden for two weeks following the 1987 floods, it continued to flower throughout. Not having done my homework, I was at first amazed at its versatility—but on looking it up I learned that it is native to *moist* meadows and light open woodland from Pennsylvania, east to Michigan and south to Florida and Texas, which obviously explained its performance in our flooded garden.

That a perennial or grass originates from the European Alps, for instance, is less than half the story. Predicting that plant's garden performance requires knowing more specific details, such as altitude above sea level, or whether a plant comes from the drier, hotter south-facing slopes or northern, shady and wetter ones. It may be an alpine, from the genus *Saxifraga*, from the high but well-drained screes; a perennial, perhaps *Trollius europaeus* from alpine meadows and streamsides; or a woodland edge grass such as *Deschampsia cespitosa*.

Exploring a plant's background can be fascinating, and it's also practical: origins have a distinct bearing on the conditions a plant will require in cultivation, and considering the plant's native topography and latitude helps us make informed garden choices. In the Directory beginning on page 78, I have tried to give insight into where some of my selected plants originate.

PREPARATION, PLANTING AND MAINTENANCE

←

Summer need never be dull with the right selection of perennials, some combined here for impact in the Summer Garden at Bressingham. *Lavandula angustifolia* 'Blue Cushion' fills the foreground, behind which are *Sedum* 'Bressingham Purple', the scarlet *Crocosmia* 'Vulcan' and, like it or not, the undeniably showy *Heliopsis helianthoides* LORAINE SUNSHINE 'Helhan'.

Is gardening pure pleasure, or is it work? Nearly always, it is a combination of the two. Few gardeners relish the harder physical work of clearing an old border of unwanted shrubs or trees, or reducing invading tree roots or perennial weeds—but it is in the careful planning as well as the ongoing processes of digging, moving compost, planting, pruning and weeding that the fun and creativity often lies. And when you prepare your garden's soil, buy plants from a garden centre, draw up a plan and develop a feasible and even satisfying maintenance routine, gardening becomes *real*. It is hard work, certainly, but with it can come great pleasure and reward.

Preparation

For the best chance of success in the garden, according to an old English proverb, "the answer lies in the soil". Thorough soil preparation is vital to success in growing all garden plants, including perennials and ornamental grasses.

Understanding Soil

Unless your garden is very small, you will probably find that soil conditions vary in different parts of the property. At Foggy Bottom, for instance, we have three types of soil on a gradual slope, the lower end of which was once a lake; we are talking about just a metre or so (a few feet) in incline. At the higher end, near our house, the rich but sticky acid clay loam is 60 cm (2 ft.) deep over sand, while in the central area there is fine loam, and in the lower area fen-like black soil that is alluvial, with close-to-neutral pH, although it is not so rich in nutrients. In some places the sand comes closer to the surface, providing better winter drainage.

Such variability in soil can be caused by a gradual or steep gradient, or equally by rubble left by a builder, closeness to a watercourse, treatment of the soil by previous occupants, a woodland area with leaf mould, a patch of impoverished sun-baked inorganic soil or numerous other factors. Some areas will vary in their acidity and alkalinity; to assess the latter, you can buy soil testing kits at most garden centres, but checking your garden (or the gardens of your neighbours) for happy-looking, acid-loving rhododendrons or azaleas will also give a clue.

For insight into whether your soil is loamy, sandy, stony, clay or a combination thereof, try digging two or three holes to a depth of 45–60 cm (1½–2 ft.) in areas where you intend to plant, when the soil is already moist. This will give you an indication of soil depth and type, but the holes will also allow you to test the drainage. If in any doubt, fill them with water; if it disappears quickly, then the drainage in the soil is fine, but if it holds water for more than half an hour, you have a problem. Perhaps there is a pan, or a hard shelf of clay, that is impeding drainage, in which case it will need to be broken up by hand-digging. (Often on clay soils a rotavator [rototiller] will create this pan by smearing the soil below the relatively shallow depth of the rotating blades.)

Like plants, soils are rarely 'perfect', but a 'medium' or alluvial, free-draining but moisture-retentive neutral loam is considered ideal for most perennials and ornamental grasses, though without conditioning few soils

Love Your Microclimates

Just as variable soil conditions can be used to advantage, allowing you to experiment with suitable plants to fit, your garden's microclimates can be seen as an opportunity rather than a problem. For instance, many perennials may be doubtfully hardy in your region, particularly in more open situations where shelter from wind and frost in winter is minimal. However, your home provides some warmth and shelter, usually on its south and west sides (north and east in the southern hemisphere), as can evergreen hedges, shrubs and trees—and the less hardy plants that require shelter and good drainage may do surprisingly well when planted in their vicinity.

When you see "dislikes winter wet" listed as a plant's cultural requirement, try planting it near the top of a slope or an incline, or on flatter ground as I often do, within reach of tree roots where the soil usually remains drier and better drained in winter. I planted the much undervalued dwarf aster, *Aster ×frikartii* 'Flora's Delight', close to the outer roots of a cedar—and although this plant normally succumbs to winter wet when young, it has been happily growing and flowering in this same place for more than six years. Alternatively, any damp or wet spot in the garden can be useful for moisture-loving plants, depending of course on whether it becomes waterlogged in winter—although even then it is always possible to find a plant to fit the conditions.

fit all of these criteria. Knowing your soil well usually takes time, and you learn as you experiment with plants. When soil varies in type and texture, this gives you a great opportunity to experiment with a wider choice of plants to fit the variable conditions.

Clearing Perennial Weeds

When you are approaching a new garden or completely replanting an old area in your garden, you should ask one question first: are there any perennial weeds such as ground elder, couch grass, bindweed or perennial thistle in the area? Answer "yes" about any of these or other perennial weeds, and of course they must be eradicated before it is safe to plant perennials and grasses.

But this is easier said than done. The most effective chemical weed killer is the systemic glyphosate which, when sprayed onto foliage, spreads through the root system to kill all parts of the plant. Glysophate should be applied in late spring or early summer, and some weeds may need a further spray later in the year, but beware: this herbicide will potentially kill any plant it touches, so great care must be taken in its application.

Digging for Success

Once perennial weeds have been cleared, other decisions must be made. If the soil is a good loam and has been planted before, it may need little more than digging, depending on the size of the area. Large areas may need ploughing or rotavating (rototilling), or both, but smaller garden plots are best hand dug. This can be hard work, or good exercise and a satisfying job, depending on

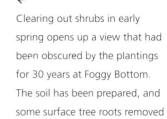

Clearing out shrubs in early spring opens up a view that had been obscured by the plantings for 30 years at Foggy Bottom. The soil has been prepared, and some surface tree roots removed from the silver birch, *Betula costata*.

←

In early summer just two years later, a 'river' of *Brunnera macrophylla* 'Jack Frost' winds through the centre of this shady area, with repeat plantings of *Hosta* 'Krossa Regal' (lifted and divided from mature clumps) and the evergreen fern *Dryopteris erythrosaura* following on either side, taking the eye to the garden seat in the distance. This combination gives interest from spring until winter, creating a vista from both sides and opening up the garden.

your age, fitness and outlook. Deeper digging will break up any hard pan and assist winter drainage. If you are working around tree roots or shrubs, now is the time to prune these a third or half way back to prevent undue competition with your perennials. Shallowly buried thick polythene sheeting can be used to line the tree side of your trench to deter feeding roots from re-invading your border, at least for a few years.

Adding Organics

If your soil is too light, too heavy or just not very fertile, then it will need the addition of organic matter such as weed-free leaf mould or compost (or, if you can get it, well-rotted farmyard manure). At Bressingham we use both of these plus composted pine bark which is also excellent as a mulch. Your compost can be mixed into your trench in the digging process, but for larger areas you may need to get a reputable landscaper to handle this operation. In all cases, thorough mixing of compost with your native garden soil is essential. Ideally soil should be prepared in late summer when conditions are neither too wet nor too dry, particularly on heavier soils, allowing the winter frosts and rain to break down the clumps of clay, with planting left until spring. In southern western-hemisphere climates where little frost and relatively little rain is experienced, autumn planting of trees, shrubs, perennials and grasses makes sense as it allows root growth to become well established before the onset of an early spring and a long, hot summer.

The Importance of Drainage

Good drainage is vital to your plants' success. In addition to the digging of holes described earlier, a quick way to test drainage is to take a cane (or similarly shaped object) into the garden, place it on the soil's surface and push: if it sinks down relatively easily to at least 45 cm (1½ ft.), and if the pan is still there, it will be necessary to re-dig, or at least to dig deeper holes, to enable seepage or runoff. If an area is really poorly drained, you may need to build a drainage system, which can be a complex and time-consuming task.

In many gardens and situations, winter wet will kill more perennials and grasses than will frost, and together the two often form a still more lethal combination. Drainage problems can be caused by using heavy machinery on large landscape projects as this will jam the soil tightly to some depth, particularly when conditions are wet. What's more, using a rotavator (rototiller) to a depth of less than 30 cm (1 ft.) will still leave a hard pan on heavier soils that roots will not be able to penetrate, and in winter neither will water, leading to poor root development and rotting.

Digging the soil and mixing in organic material will help to open up clay soil and retain necessary moisture on very free-draining types. Planting beds can be mounded into attractive forms that improve drainage along with adding interest to flat landscapes; although the higher levels of planting may require more irrigation in summer, at least this gives you the opportunity to plant those perennials and grasses that dislike winter wet in more favourable conditions. On heavy soils that (ideally) should not be stepped on in the wet of winter, it is a good idea to create steps or pathways to allow access to plants so that you can weed and cut back without exacerbating drainage problems.

Planting

When you buy your plants, this is when the excitement can really begin. Except when ordered by mail, perennials and grasses are mostly sold in pots of various sizes. Some perennials in particular can grow quite quickly, and if you are on a tight budget, the plants in smaller pots will be well established by late summer if planted in spring. Larger pot sizes and plants will make more immediate impact, and are probably best used from midsummer onwards. These plants should be more mature, have a larger root mass to establish quickly, and are less likely to heave or lift during autumn and winter frosts. They are also easier to water and have more reserves for summer planting.

Bare root or open-ground plants are still offered by some retail outlets and mail order companies. Traditionally, perennial stalwarts such as *Paeonia*, *Iris* and *Hemerocallis* (daylilies) have been sold as bare root plants in late summer and autumn, and this is still a fine practice if nursery plants are carefully and quickly handled, but unfortunately with several moves from nursery beds to your garden, sometimes across an ocean, bare root plants can deteriorate badly and will take some time to recover (if recovery is even possible). Try to deal only with a reputable nursery company that grows its own open-ground plants. Lifting, dividing and replanting from specimens grown in your own garden is a different matter, and this subject is covered later in this chapter.

Expect the Best, Prepare for Less

We expect a lot from our new plants, and with good preparation and aftercare they do not usually disappoint. When collecting from a garden centre or when plants are delivered, carefully check for freedom from weeds, clear labelling and general quality. Good-quality plants should be well rooted around the pot, and during the growing season the foliage should look healthy. If your perennials and grasses are not fully rooted, handle with care when planting: prepare the hole and try to keep all the soil and roots together as you plant in one motion. On the other extreme, if plants have dense, tightly congested roots, you may need to cut some away at the base of the plant with a sharp knife or at least prise apart the lower roots around the base with a hand fork or, on larger plants, a digging fork. This work should be undertaken just before planting begins so that roots do not dry out. If any are dry, keep them well watered and then soak them thoroughly in a bucket for 10 to 15 minutes before planting.

Be Creative in Setting Out and Spacing

Assuming that the soil in your bed has been prepared and the border perimeters defined with grass, paving or pathways, and that you will be planting an empty bed or around trees and shrubs (whether already-existing or simply planned), now is the time to set the date for setting out your plants. Unless you are diligently following someone else's plan, you are the artist, and this will be your creation. After all of the preparation, it will feel pretty good to get to this stage.

Even if your plan looks great on paper, you may find that

→

In the new Summer Garden at
Bressingham, the perennials
in pots have been set out and
spring planting begins. Summer
colour is a main aim. The other is
to display the National Collection
of *Miscanthus* with other plants.

→

A year and a half later, the
view in late summer towards
Bressingham Hall has been
transformed by the quick-to-
establish perennials and grasses
growing in soil that had been a
meadow for over 50 years.

it does not look right in the context of the garden's actual dimensions, views and aspects—so once your last plants are placed you can finalize any adjustments before planting. In general, the space around shrubs, conifers or specimen trees should be much wider than the space between individual perennials and grasses unless you plan to plant beneath woody plants as ground cover. Consider using perennials such as *Eupatorium maculatum* 'Gateway' or grasses such as *Miscanthus sinensis* 'Morning Light', allowing them to stand out above their neighbours. Also consider lower drifts or 'rivers' of plants like *Geranium* 'Rozanne' to add intrigue and drama to your planting, and above all think carefully about the periods of interest you can create through the year. Actual spacing needs to be worked out according to the height and width expected in the growth of the plant. The lower and smaller the plant, of course, the closer together they should be planted. For all of the perennials and ornamental grasses in the Directory, I have noted expected height and width after three years' growth from young plants.

The Process of Planting

With soil prepared, plants soaked, weeds removed and space ready for planting, it is time to pick up the trowel, hand fork and spade and let the planting begin. Remove the pot and open or trim up any congested roots, create the hole, insert your plant to the same level, pull the soil back around the plant and firm: simple steps, of course, but a few tips are worth considering according to planting conditions.

It is best to avoid planting when it is raining or very wet, particularly on heavier clay soils, as the soil will compact when stepping on the surface or when firming in your plants. On our heavier soil areas in Foggy Bottom, I avoid planting in such conditions but if I must, I use boards which can be moved around as I plant, supporting and spreading the impact of my weight. On lighter soils and in drier conditions, firm in your plants with either a hand on either side of the plant or with your foot. On heavier soils and with moister conditions, avoid such heavy firming. Work backwards from the furthest point from the bed edge to avoid treading on planted soil. If compacted, prick up the surface as you retreat, so that any smearing of the surface will not impede drainage.

Watering and Irrigation

In these environmentally conscious times we should all look to ways to use water efficiently in our gardens, ideally using no more than necessary. Unless you have a highly organized automatic system with pipes feeding individual drip feed to containers, hanging baskets and window boxes and pop-up sprinklers in the garden, watering can be quite a time-consuming job. Apart from only growing drought-resistant plants in the open ground, there are ways to help plants get established quickly and to retain moisture for a longer period, reducing the need for constant watering.

One way is to prepare the soil with additional organic material, dug or mixed in to at least 30 cm (1 ft.), to give plants nourishment and moisture in depth. After planting, watering the plants individually using a watering can or an extended lance at the end of a hose binds the moisture from roots to new soil. Additionally, adding 5–7.5 cm (about 3 in.) of mulch around each plant or, better still, the whole bed will hold the moisture in and prevent a mass of annual weeds from appearing.

For general irrigation with sprinklers, night time is the most efficient, although recent trials have shown that this is not always the best practice for some plants prone to damping off, for which early morning watering may be better. Depending on the time of the year and the weather, regular irrigation will be more necessary for new plantings than for older ones whose root systems are more established.

The Advantages of Mulch

Mulch: a nice word, but what does it mean? In simple terms it is merely a covering placed on the surface of cultivated soil. It can take the form leaf mould, composted bark, coconut shells, stone or gravel and should of course be sterile or free of weed seeds—even though, once down, the mulch can act as a fertile bed for plants or weeds to seed in. In recent years the term 'mulch' has come to be applied to less natural materials such as polythene or plastic sheeting through which plants can be inserted. The mulch is there to retain moisture during dry periods and to prevent annual weeds from growing, and of course all weeds should be removed prior to mulching anyway. An organic mulch will keep soils cooler and will allow better root development.

Using organic material immediately after planting has many benefits. At Bressingham we mostly use a fine or medium grade composted pine bark, but it is important to ask your local garden centre or contractor what is available and recommended for your garden. We put the compost on with large pots or buckets so that it can be heaped between the plants and then spread by hand to create a smooth surface.

Make sure not to bury the plants too deeply in compost, as in wet conditions this can cause the plants to damp off. Late winter or spring is a good time to mulch, but any summer plantings will also benefit, and an early autumn mulch can also be used to protect less hardy plants by retaining soil warmth longer and reducing later frost penetration. Be aware, though, that if a thick layer of mulch dries out in summer above a dry soil, it will take repeated watering to re-soak. It is of course not cheap to mulch your garden on a regular basis, but it is of definite benefit. Composting your own leaf mould, even topping up your supply with your neighbours' if they have no use for it, is a satisfying and economical alternative. On your second and consecutive mulch additions, it is a good idea to lightly fork over the previously mulched surface so it blends in with the soil prior to spreading on your new mulch.

Maintenance

Planting and mulching done: now time to sit back and enjoy? Of course it is, but haven't we already enjoyed the planning, (some of the) preparation, planting and mulching too?

As you watch your own creation grow, you will need to keep an eye on any watering requirements and remove annual or perennial weeds as soon as they appear. In your first year there should be little maintenance beyond this,

→

After spring flowers have finished, pulmonarias should at least have their stems and potential seedheads cut away. In the case of *P.* 'Diana Clare' and other forms with good summer foliage, a more thorough trimming and cleaning is required. The new leaves will then make foliage to last all summer.

but your enjoyment will come from observation and learning.

It is an excellent idea to label your plants, whether the label is easily visible or not, and ideally to draw yourself a plan after planting, indicating where each group, species or cultivar is planted. Learning the names of plants is to learn about horticulture. And each plant has a history. From which continent did it originate and under what conditions does it grow? Who discovered it and when? Who was the breeder, or was it just a chance seedling found by an amateur? How does my experience of growing it compare with the descriptions in various books, catalogues and references?

We are all are bound to enjoy some aspects of gardening more than others, but it is vital to leave time for the pleasure of wandering around your newly created or established garden on a summer evening with a glass of wine in your hand, or just sitting and watching the magic of nature.

Maintenance Priority in the Ongoing Garden

My father Alan Bloom once wrote a book called *Perennials for Trouble Free Gardening* that suggested a list of perennials needing less attention or maintenance than most; at that time (in the 1960s) he suggested that they were much less trouble than annuals. 'Trouble free' is of course a relative term and in reality, unless you are happy with a totally wild garden, no garden is completely free of trouble. Weeds need weeding, grass and lawns need mowing, trees, conifers, shrubs and hedges need pruning, annuals need renewing each year and perennials and ornamental grasses need some attention. Once again, part of the gardening experience and enjoyment is the maintenance of the plants within it.

Maintenance of perennials and grasses includes watering and mulching as necessary and keeping your plants happy and thriving. Some may fade away and need replacing with more of the same or with something else, others will grow too vigorously and may need curbing once a year or so, and many will lose vigour and diminish in flowering performance after a few years because they become too congested. The latter, including many asters, *Phlox paniculata*, *Leucanthemum*, *Monarda* and even astilbes and hostas, will need dividing, retaining the youngest and healthiest part of the group and then replanting in improved soil conditions. Other options are to manage your perennials more innovatively such as by pruning or trimming to reduce height or spread, to delay flowering, to prune after a first flush of flower to encourage a later-season repeat performance, and of course to carry out the rather tiresome task of deadheading stalwarts like *Hemerocallis*. Many of these practices have been used for years by some gardeners, but credit should be given to Tracy DiSabato-Aust whose detailed coverage of planting and pruning techniques in her 1998 book *The Well-Tended Perennial Garden* filled a much-needed gap for the perennial gardener. This is a book by an American landscape designer and gardener from Ohio in the American midwest, but most of the information is equally useful to gardeners across the globe wherever perennials are grown. Of course, you can also turn to the Directory on page 78 for specific cultural advice on a selection of perennials.

→

In late winter, before new foliage emerges in spring, the last of the miscanthus and panicum should be cut to the ground. When cutting many plants, hedge trimmers or a strimmer are quicker alternatives to secateurs or hand pruners. Here *Miscanthus sinensis* 'Morning Light' is being cut down in Foggy Bottom.

I cannot help wondering whether we have now come full circle with our attitude towards perennials' maintenance requirements. From labour-intensive Victorian and early 20th century times, to a more relaxed view of how perennials could be used during the mid to later part of the century, we can now make perennials and grasses as labour-intensive as we want. Whatever level of maintenance we choose to follow, perennials are indispensable in providing the missing ingredient in our gardens, integrating their tremendous diversity of flower and foliage to fit almost any space.

A Calendar of Cutting Back

Since the majority of plants described in the Directory are given detailed cultural recommendations, this section will give a broader seasonal approach, starting with mid spring, as the new growth is beginning to take off, all of the previous year's foliage having now been cut back. The spent flowers and foliage of early-spring-flowering perennials like pulmonarias and brunneras are best cut back in mid spring to prevent seeding and to allow new leaves to develop. *Brunnera macrophylla* 'Jack Frost' and *Pulmonaria* 'Diana Clare' in particular have foliage to rival any hosta and should have any old or disfigured leaves removed to allow clean new leaves to emerge. The growth surge in late spring soon brings on early summer flowers such as hardy geraniums, campanulas, *Nepeta* and *Salvia nemorosa*, and call for a summer cut back once the main flowering has finished, to allow re-blooming later in the summer. (This varies by species and cultivar, so please check details in the Directory.) Some perennials, such as the oriental poppies, *Papaver orientale*, need cutting back severely after flowering, which leaves a gap that is seldom filled by another flower for the rest of the year; although briefly spectacular, they therefore do not make my shortlist.

Mid to late summer is the time to deadhead, removing flowers that have finished. This will help to prolong blooming as well as keeping groups clean and attractive for longer. Summer-flowering hardy geraniums can be cleaned up and old flowering stems cut away, but avoid being too drastic.

In autumn, unless plants look scruffy or have collapsed due to heavy rain or wind, there is no need to rush to cut back. Enjoy the gradual dying back of the flowers and foliage of both perennials and grasses; with the lowering autumn sun and perhaps the first frosts, light now begins to play an increasingly important role in the garden. As grasses turn gold then beige, some, such as taller *Miscanthus* or *Molinia caerulea* cultivars, are easily blown over and are best cut back. In late autumn and into winter, tidy up perennials if desired, but leave some such as echinaceas, sedums, monardas and *Verbena bonariense* to display their winter seedheads. Leave grasses like *Pennisetum alopecuroides* 'Hameln', *Deschampsia cespitosa*, *Miscanthus sinensis* 'Morning Light', *Panicum virgatum* 'Northwind' and *Hakonechloa macra* until late winter or even early spring, when they should be cut back fairly hard before new growth begins. Exceptions include *Sedum spectabile* 'Matrona' and 'Herbstfreude', whose old flowerheads still remain attractive as succulent new shoots appear and cutting back can be delayed for a few more weeks.

The timing of the final cleanup of old flowers, foliage

↑

Trimming or pruning perennials can alter their height, width and flowering time. In this case at Foggy Bottom, *Monarda didyma* 'Jacob Cline' is growing vigorously and will soon hide the variegated *Cornus alba* 'Halo' in the centre.

↗

By trimming around the group with shears in early summer, lower at the front than the back, the cornus can be an important part of the association when it comes into flower later in the summer, as the monarda is taller at the back than the front. →

and leaves is a matter of choice, but is best done prior to new growth beginning. In the smaller garden, all you will need is a sharp pair of secateurs or shears that let you get close-up and personal with your plants, which is part of the enjoyment (unless the plant in question is, for instance, a thorny *Berberis*). In larger gardens or landscapes, use a strimmer or a motorized or electric hedge trimmer.

Playing with Perennials

At times we may just wish to adjust height, appearance or flowering of our plants through trimming or pruning. To this end, I recommend 'playing' with perennials; after all, if we can prune a yew or beech into a hedge or topiary, why shouldn't we also manipulate perennials to make them more effective in our gardens?

For instance, in North America *Leucanthemum ×superbum* 'Becky' is considered to be the best performer and mostly grows to 90 cm. (3 ft.) or so—while in England, with longer springs and cooler summers, it grows to 150 cm (5 ft.) before it flowers. Yet I found that cutting it halfway back with shears in late spring delays flowering by a couple of weeks, and then it only reaches a more manageable 120 cm (4 ft.). Other perennials such as *Monarda* 'Jacob Cline', *Helianthus* 'Lemon Queen', *Eupatorium maculatum* 'Gateway' and *Phlox paniculata* can be treated similarly: although flowers may be smaller and later, the plants will be shorter. These methods are outlined in more detail under the individual plants' Directory entries. That these plants respond so readily to our actions in the garden is a reminder that we can experiment more freely to make them fit our gardens' size or situation.

Divide and Rule

Some vigorous perennials and ornamental grasses have running root systems that invade other plants, and

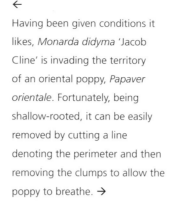

← Having been given conditions it likes, *Monarda didyma* 'Jacob Cline' is invading the territory of an oriental poppy, *Papaver orientale*. Fortunately, being shallow-rooted, it can be easily removed by cutting a line denoting the perimeter and then removing the clumps to allow the poppy to breathe. →

these thugs are best avoided. Yet other quick-spreading perennials and grasses are less invasive and, being highly ornamental, may be desirable. In such cases—examples include *Monarda*, *Anemone hybrida*, *Artemisia ludoviciana* 'Valerie Finnis' and *Achillea millefolium* hybrids— you must be prepared to curb their enthusiastic habits. In poorer or drier soils growth may be less vigorous, while moister, lighter soils will encourage vigour. There is unlikely to be much of a problem in the first year after planting, but thereafter a late winter or early spring curb can be made by cutting away the outward growth, with possibly a further check or two being made later in the growing season. Some of these perennials will spread on their outer perimeter to conquer new territory while dying out in the middle the spot where they were originally planted; in this case, discard the old material, dig in some fresh compost and then replant with a clump of younger material.

Many other perennials and ornamental grasses have a slow spreading habit and may only need dividing every few years, but some of these can also be curbed as long as vigour remains in the centre of the plant. Among grasses, examples include *Miscanthus sinensis* cultivars, *Cortaderia selloana*, *Pumila* and *Panicum virgatum*, while perennials in this category include *Eupatorium maculatum* 'Gateway', some asters and heleniums, *Phlox paniculata* and *Leucanthemum maximum* cultivars, to name a few. Even hostas can become too large. But aside from curbing vigour, dividing old groups of plants can serve to increase them to make a larger planting, as gifts for friends, or even to start a nursery!

If older groups of perennials need reinvigorating, lift all the plants at the appropriate time and either divide them on the spot in a barrow or move them to where you have more space. Select the most vigorous small clumps the size of your fist to replant and, if not required, discard or compost the remainder. If you intend to replant in the same position, add well-rotted weed-free compost and dig in prior to planting. Generally few perennials or grasses require additional fertilizer if soil conditions are right.

Lifting and dividing larger clumps will need energy and muscle, but also technique. I dislike cutting off more fibrous roots than necessary, but to actually lift a large miscanthus or hosta, both best carried out in late winter or early spring, you will need to cut around the clump with a sharp spade, severing the spreading roots. Using a spade or a strong fork, lever the clump in its hole onto its side, find a point between stems and soon-to-emerge shoots and insert two garden forks as deeply as possible, back to back so steel meets with steel. Then lever apart, if necessary inserting the forks even more deeply as you proceed. Keeping the plant halfway in the hole keeps it steadier than above ground and a sideways division does less harm to developing buds or shoots. Now, with two large divisions, repeat the process to divide further, bearing in mind that the first cut is the hardest. Straggly roots can be trimmed before planting, but not too short. For small plants and divisions I like to use two small hand forks back to back, and occasionally a curved propagating knife if more surgical-style division is required.

←

Miscanthus sinensis 'Morning Light' is extremely tough to lift and divide, but it can be done. After cutting back old foliage in late winter, cut around the outer roots with a sharp spade.

→

Then put in two large garden forks back to back and lever the loosened clump apart by pushing the handles outward, putting the forks in gradually deeper until the clump divides.

←

If any resistance is still present, lever one half of the clump away from the other. Remove the first division and repeat to make smaller divisions if required.

→

Dividing a clump on its side in the hole is sometimes even more effective if it is not too heavy to assume that position. This method becomes more necessary when new shoots have already begun. In order not to damage emerging hosta buds, two forks should split from the side and slightly below the shoots to avoid breaking them.

→

Lastly, for smaller clumps, using two hand forks may be more appropriate, as on this clump of *Coreopsis verticillata* 'Zagreb'.

DIRECTORY OF
RECOMMENDED PERENNIALS
AND GRASSES

A ten-year-old group of the
outstanding *Agapanthus* 'Loch
Hope' surrounds the erect reddish
plumes of *Miscanthus sinensis*
'Ferner Osten' in early autumn in
Foggy Bottom, Bressingham.

The plants profiled here, of course, cannot be expected to succeed under all conditions. However, I believe that they can be considered among the best in their genera. As a gardener and nurseryman who has witnessed so many new selections becoming available only to be proven less-than-gardenworthy, I consider my selection very much to fall under the 'tried-and-tested' label, having been introduced and trialled widely in gardens for a decade or more, proving themselves over time.

This is not a comprehensive encyclopedia; by reducing the selection, I have been able to give more background and cultural information about those I have selected. As discussed earlier, a plant's origins can give great insight into its preferences, helping to predict how it might perform in your garden. What's more, it is interesting—exciting, even—to think that many species and hybrids found in the garden have their roots all over the world. Many hybrids and cultivars arose by luck or by chance, but often with the help of breeders.

At the end of each main plant description you will find the plant's estimated dimensions (height and expected spread or width after three years, in that order), a general flowering period (for instance, spring or summer) and hardiness zone information.

In North America, which has such variable climatic regions, the United States Department of Agriculture (USDA) has produced a guide and map to indicate the zones of likely winter temperatures, and all garden plants have been assigned a hardiness category: the lower the figure, the hardier the plant. This is only a guide, since climates are undoubtedly changing, and as many experienced gardeners will know, most of us have warmer microclimates in parts of our gardens. Heat and humidity tolerance is equally important to gardeners in many regions. Most descriptions indicate where a plant may be susceptible to such conditions, and additionally the higher number in the zone range indicates a plant's tolerance for heat. *Phlox paniculata* cultivars, for instance are hardy to zone 4 from Vermont in the north and have heat tolerance to zone 9 in the southern state of Louisiana. When we consider, however, that the United Kingdom is mostly in hardiness zones 8 and 9, the same as the American states of Georgia and Mississippi—although England's summer climate is vastly different from these southern U.S. states'—it becomes clear that these figures can only be used as a rough guide. For a zone temperature table, see page 198.

Not enough choice? With around 400 selections of of perennials and grasses described, this book is hardly without variety, but as a gardener you may find that your own top-performing or favourite plant happens to lie outside these pages. At any rate, I hope that this Directory of proven performers helps you to navigate the dizzying choice available. If the first part of the book offers ideas and inspiration, this Directory gives you the opportunity to put ideas into practice with an excellent range of reliable plants. My ultimate goal is to enable more people to enjoy the benefits of gardening, and I hope that this Directory will encourage you to do just that.

Imposing spikes of purple hooded flowers rise above sharply pointed deep green leaves of *Acanthus spinosus* in summer in Foggy Bottom.

be sited carefully, perhaps against a wall or on a bank, and it will take part shade too although it may flower less. Once the leaves have died back after autumn frosts you will have a long period where a patch of bare soil with no sign of life is evident until the late spring of the following year. Though only hardy to zone 7, given spring planting and an appropriate position a hardier rating even to zone 5 could be expected. Small plants can be slow to establish and are best planted in spring in colder regions. A winter protection of a leafy mulch can be given 5–10 cm (2–4 in.) deep as long as good drainage exists beneath.

120 cm (4 ft.) × 60–90 cm (2–3 ft.)

F summer

Z 7–9

Further Recommendations

A. hungaricus (syn. *A. longifolius*) is reliably free-flowering and has white or light pink, purple hooded flowers on tall 120–150-cm (4–5-ft.) spikes, with long narrow dull green leaves up to 1 m (3 ft.) long. **Z** 6–9.

Acanthus spinosus

bear's breeches, spiny bear's breeches

Although not always easy to place in the garden, *A. spinosus* is an impressive foliage and flowering perennial.

Native to eastern Italy, the Balkans and Turkey, it has deep fleshy tap roots and from spring to late autumn forms a handsome mound of long arching, dark glossy green, deeply cut, white-veined leaves edged with spines, though these are not sharp. The spiny reputation applies to the foxglove-like flowers borne on 120-cm (4-ft.) spikes from early summer. These white flowers, capped with purple bracts, nestle above a green bract that terminates in a needle-sharp point. They give a summer-long display and are good for cutting and drying.

As might be guessed from its origins, *A. spinosus* likes a sunny, warm, well-drained position, disliking winter wet. This species, once established, has a robust spreading habit and so should

→
Silver-grey leaves and cheerfully bright lemon-yellow flowers of *Achillea* 'Moonshine' highlight the centre of Richard Ayres's colourful cottage garden in Cambridgeshire, England on a midsummer day.

Achillea 'Moonshine'

yarrow

We are still looking for the perfect achillea, but *A*. 'Moonshine', with its bright summer foliage and even brighter, cheerful early flowers, comes pretty close.

One of many seedlings of the grey-leaved *A. clypeolata* raised by my father Alan Bloom around 1950, it displayed wonderful silvery grey foliage but no flower in its position beneath an old apple tree at Bressingham. But once moved to an open sunny position, the seedling soon to become 'Moonshine' flowered profusely.

It is aptly named for its flat heads of cheerful bright lemon yellow flowers over silvery grey finely cut foliage. Ideally it needs good drainage, but will grow on heavier soils. Clumps are best divided every two or three years in early autumn or spring to maintain youth, vigour and flower performance. In late spring or early summer, 'Moonshine' makes a brilliant contrast to *Salvia* ×*sylvestris* 'Mainacht' (in English, 'May Night'), and will continue to flower on and off later in summer if old dead heads are cut away.

60 cm (2 ft.) × 45 cm (1½ ft.)
F summer
Z 3–8

Further Recommendations
It is difficult to see any influence of *A. millefolium* in 'Moonshine', but this is certainly evident in another selection raised 30 years later and named by my father for my stepsister Anthea, which is arguably a longer-lived perennial. *A.* ANTHEA 'Anblo' may be less spectacular than 'Moonshine', but it is also less likely to 'melt out' in hot humid climates. At 60 cm (2 ft.) with grey-green foliage and paler soft yellow flowers on more erect stems, it will repeat-flower into the autumn if old flowers are removed. Other sturdy varieties with distinctive flat heads of deep yellow are *A. millefolium* 'Coronation Gold', 90 cm (3 ft.), an English hybrid introduced in 1952 and named for Queen Elizabeth's Coronation, and the spectacular and well-named *A. filipendulina* 'Gold Plate', with

↑

With flattened yellow-centred orange flowers, *Achillea* 'Walter Funcke' makes a bold splash in early summer, contrasting with the pale blue flowers of *Geranium* 'Blue Cloud' in the Dell Garden at Bressingham.

large flat heads of mustard yellow on tall sturdy unbranched 150–180-cm (5–6-ft.) stems. All are good for cutting and drying. All **Z** 4–8.

Although the species *A. millefolium* (milfoil), which has many herbal properties, has become naturalized in North America, it is actually native to Europe and much of Asia, spreading by roots and seed. Recent hybridizing has produced some colourful and attractive cultivars that add much to the palette of the summer garden. Most have green or grey-green fern-like finely divided foliage, rough to the touch, with heights varying from 30 to 120 cm (1–4 ft.) and flattish flower-heads carrying small, two-toned flowers of an amazing range, from pink to red, yellow to orange and everything in between. Some cultivars fade ignominiously to grey, others to more pleasing subtle shades. They are ideal for sunny well-drained sites, although many are aggressive, particularly in moist soils and cooler climates, and will need controlling, while others die out if too wet in winter. These are high-maintenance plants that will give a longer flowering performance if cut back by half after the first main bloom. Look for orange-yellow 'Terracotta', 90–120 cm (3–4 ft.), and orange-red 'Walther Funcke', shorter at 30–60 cm (1–2 ft.), both raised by German plantsman Ernst Pagels. 'Summerwine', 60–90 cm (2–3 ft.) is purple-red, and there will be further introduction of new cultivars. Do not allow these plants to self-seed.

Aconitum carmichaelii 'Arendsii'

monkshood

A wonderful late show of almost-cobalt-blue flowers to combine and contrast with autumn colours makes this a worthy choice.

Originally selected in 1945 by Georg Arends in Germany, this plant is chosen for its very late display of glistening deep blue hooded flowers on strong 120-cm (4-ft.) spikes, which make a striking contrast to the autumnal hues of various grasses and shrubs.

'Arendsii' provides ample glossy foliage through the summer, developing flower buds up the stems, opening in early autumn from the top and gradually moving down, giving a long and vibrant display. The height may vary considerably according to soil type and degree of moisture, and plants can freely seed in appropriate conditions.

Although aconitums are rightly described as poisonous, this is only a concern if they are eaten: they are toxic if ingested. Not suitable for every garden, they prefer a reasonably moist organic soil and, in hotter regions, at least part shade. Most aconitums grow

←
The deep blue hooded flowers of *Aconitum carmichaelii* 'Arendsii' always bring valuable and striking late colour to the autumn garden.

→
A carpet of the golden variegated dwarf sweetflag, *Acorus gramineus* 'Oborozuki', contrasts with bronze midwinter hues of *Microbiota decussata*, a conifer from Siberia, in the Winter Garden at Bressingham.

from a tuberous rootstock and may want dividing every few years. This is best done in autumn, but when handling any part of the plant it is best to use gloves and wash hands thoroughly afterwards. The dark green lobed leaves and flowers are very distinctive, and once established they are very easy to grow, making excellent plants for sun or light shade, with a long display of striking flowers.

120–150 cm (4–5 ft.) × 30 cm (1 ft.)

F autumn

Z 3–8

Further Recommendations

Back in the late 1950s, my father Alan Bloom selected and raised two distinctive monkshoods that are still worthwhile garden plants. *Aconitum* 'Bressingham Spire' is a classic—tuberous, with finely cut deep green leaves and an erectly branched tapering habit to 90–120 cm (3–4 ft.), needing no staking, and violet-blue flowers in mid to late summer. 'Blue Sceptre' has a similar erect habit but is shorter, its glossy green leaves setting off the blue and white flowers on 60–75-cm (2–2½-ft.) stems. Both **Z** 4–8.

Acorus gramineus 'Oborozuki'

dwarf sweetflag

This evergreen or evergold grass-like perennial is indispensable in the year-round garden, and much more adaptable than is often recognized.

The species, one of only two in the genus, is found across a widespread area stretching from India to China, Siberia and Japan, mostly inhabiting moist or boggy places. *A. gramineus* forms clumps of spreading rhizomes, with glossy, dark green arching fans of grassy foliage, making good ground cover in sun or light shade where not too dry.

'Oborozuki', one of a few selections with gold or variegated foliage, is brightness itself, particularly welcome in winter, its narrow pointed green-edged leaves a bright gold even in semi-shade. Though often described as needing very moist or boggy conditions, 'Oborozuki' is adaptable to a wide range of soils, except where it is too dry in which case the scorched leaf tips will indicate that it needs a moister position. 'Oborozuki' is also

sold as an evergreen houseplant. Flowers are insignificant, if there are any.

Plants divide easily in early spring or summer, and the roots should be planted slightly deeper and firmed well in, mulching with leaf mould or composted bark to retain moisture. Sometimes it is confused with (and sold under the name of) 'Ogon'; you can recognize 'Oborozuki' by its light green stripes, while 'Ogon' has purely golden leaves.

30–45 cm (1–1½ ft.) × 30–45 cm (1–1½ ft.)

F early summer

Z 5–9

Actaea simplex 'Brunette'

simple stem bugbane

'Brunette' is a wonderful perennial with a long period of interest, from spring when new shoots unfurl from a woody rootstock until well into autumn, with fragrant flowers on tall arching spikes.

The species *A. simplex* (syn. *A. ramosa*) is native to northern Japan, Korea,

←
Striking all summer long, the purple leaves of *Actaea simplex* 'Brunette' are enhanced by graceful bottlebrush heads of fragrant flowers in late summer and autumn. Dell Garden, Bressingham.

season of interest, with seedheads remaining attractive. Like most actaeas, 'Brunette' is easily grown given a well-composted or organic soil that does not dry out. As most actaeas originate in cooler parts of the northern hemisphere, they are best in full sun or half shade according to climate. Division is best done in spring, but these plants prefer not to be disturbed too often.

150–180 cm (5–6 ft.) × 60–75 cm (2–2½ ft.)

F late summer and autumn

Z 6–8

Further Recommendations

'Brunette' has two close competitors, whose supporters believe they are superior in leaf colour—but you would need to see *A. simplex* 'Hillside Black Beauty', raised in New England, and *A. simplex* 'James Compton' (named in Holland after the English plantsman who was largely responsible for revising the genus from *Cimicifuga* into *Actaea*), growing right next to 'Brunette' to notice any difference. Both are excellent perennials similar in size and flowering time to 'Brunette'. The close relation *A. matsumurae* has at least two

northeastern China and into Russia and Siberia, so we can be confident of its hardiness. The less-than-complimentary common name of bugbane applies to the properties in some species which allegedly keep insects at bay. 'Brunette' was selected in the 1980s by Danish nurserywoman H. Christiansen of Virum Planteskole from seedlings of the variable *A. s.* 'Atropurpurea'; on a visit to her nursery I was delighted to obtain plants to introduce it to British gardeners in 1990.

The new, finely divided leaves emerge a deep, almost black-purple, and in a semi-shady spot will remain deep purple for most of the summer at 60–90 cm (2–3 ft.) high, perhaps fading in more open positions as flowering spikes develop in late summer and early autumn. From ground level these graceful, black waving stems can reach 150–180 cm (5–6 ft.), terminating in bottlebrush heads, purple-pink in bud, opening to white and heavily fragrant flowers, the culmination of a long

→

Agapanthus 'Loch Hope' makes a dramatic show in the Dell Garden at Bressingham, displaying large heads with deep blue flowers that last for many weeks in late summer. At 120–150 cm (4–5 ft.) they tower above the shorter *Phlox paniculata* 'Bright Eyes'.

selections worth mentioning, being shorter and very arching in habit, and flowering in very late autumn. *A. m.* 'Elstead' is my favourite, with brown-black stems, brown diffused leaves and flower buds opening to white-petalled flowers: very graceful and distinctive. *A. m.* 'White Pearl' has pale green leaves and pure white flowers. Both reach 90–150 cm (3–5 ft.), depending on moisture and situation.

Agapanthus 'Loch Hope'

African lily

Choosing from a multitude of excellent cultivars of the African lily, I recommend 'Loch Hope' for its stature, its late- and long-flowering performance and its hardiness.

Agapanthus originate from South Africa and the question of hardiness probably arises from the broad-leaved evergreen species that were first imported to Europe, such as *A. africanus*, which came from lower and coastal areas and often ended up as exotics for conservatories and summer terraces. The deciduous species with narrower leaves, mainly *A. campanulatus* and *A. inapertus*, grow at higher

and cooler altitudes in eastern South Africa and Lesotho, and are much hardier. The meaning of the term 'hardy', of course, depends on where you live and garden, but once established and with careful siting (and maybe some winter protection), 'Loch Hope' and other cultivars recommended below would grow successfully in USDA hardiness zone 7 or even 6.

Raised and introduced in 1974 at the Savill Gardens in Windsor by former curator John Bond, and named after a Scottish lake, it will not disappoint. Like all African lilies, it has a clump-forming, fleshy rootstock, from which emerge quite broad, 3-cm (1-in.) wide dark green overlapping leaves to 30 cm (1 ft.). It is not until late summer that round flowering stems emerge, reaching full height before the flowers open. The deep violet-blue buds are tightly held in a papery capsule, slowly breaking out from one side to form a head of up to 70 dark violet-blue flowers that last for weeks into autumn, followed by attractive seedheads.
120–150 cm (4–5 ft.) × 45–60 cm (1½–2 ft.)

F late summer, autumn

Z 7–9

Further Recommendations

Since they have become such popular plants, and are easily grown from seed, far too many *Aganthus* cultivars have been introduced in recent years. While some are not worthy of garden space, particularly those offered as seedlings, certain ones will not disappoint. If blue seems the true colour of agapanthus (and I much prefer them to the whites) I recommend that you follow 'Loch Hope' with the free-flowering 'Bressingham Blue', 90 cm (3 ft.) tall; the Bressingham-raised 'Isis', 60 cm (2 ft.) tall; and the slightly tender 'Lilliput' 30–45 cm (1–1½ ft.) tall, which all have deep violet-blue flowers in summer in proportion with the plant, the latter two being excellent for pots or containers. Becoming more popular and widely available are the *Agapanthus inapertus* species and cultivars, whose stems (or peduncles) are often rigidly upright, bearing heads of pendulous flowers from deep, almost black-purple-blue (if such a colour combination is possible), to pale-blue and even white. These and other agapanthus are excellent cut flowers and in the garden mix well with those other South African summer stalwarts, crocosmias and kniphofias.

←

Although the flowers of *Alchemilla mollis* may be relatively short lived, they make an imposing display at their peak here in early summer, with tiny chartreuse blooms above the large bright green leaves. When flowers collapse (as they will), cut them back to enjoy ground-covering foliage for the rest of summer and autumn.

Alchemilla mollis

lady's mantle

Although dismissed by some gardeners as too weedy, *A. mollis* is a good and reliable perennial I would not be without.

One of nearly 300 *Alchemilla* species, this member of the rose family (who would have thought it?) comes from southeastern Europe, Turkey and the Caucasus where it grows in open meadows, along streamsides and in light woodland, often at considerable altitude. With the largest leaves in the genus—15 cm (6 in.) across—it makes an attractive ground cover plant with a long period of interest. Aside from a tendency to seed freely in suitable conditions, it has very few faults.

Plants form sturdy, mounded clumps. The broad-lobed light green leaves are hairy on both sides, with finely serrated edges. One of the marvels of the lady's mantle is caused by the hairs on the surface, holding sparkling dewdrops on the leaves on summer mornings. For a short time in early summer the sprays of chartreuse flowers smother the plant, transforming its appearance, but once these begin to fade and brown, they are best cut away, the foliage remaining attractive until autumn. If leaves do look messy, cut back but not too hard in late summer and new foliage will appear.

In cooler climates these are plants for sun or shade where not too dry, though they are survivors even in such places. Leaves may scorch where plants are too hot and dry in summer. Cutting back flowers will prevent seeding, but unwanted seedlings should be dug out of patio paving and other niches before they get too big. *A. mollis* is a very useful plant for many positions in gravel, patio or courtyards, as edging for a pathway, beneath deciduous shrubs, and in association with other spring-flowering perennials where it can soften bright colours.

30–45 cm (1–1½ ft.) × 45–60 cm (1½–2 ft.)

F summer

Z 4–7

→
North American native *Amsonia tabernaemontana* var. *salicifolia*, is shown in late spring in the Dell Garden, Bressingham. The species is similar in most respects, but has broader leaves.

Amsonia tabernaemontana

blue star

An understated but reliable perennial, *Amsonia tabernaemontana* is exquisite in flower, with attractive foliage from spring until autumn.

It is one of about 20 species in this genus of hardy perennials, most of which are native to North America. *A. tabernaemontana* is found growing in moist soils in open grassland and on roadsides, woodland edges and stream banks from New Jersey to Florida and across to Illinois and Texas. In spring, from a semi-woody rootstock, distinctive purple-black stems appear, forming a clump of matt green willow-like leaves. Heads of dark blue buds open to bright, pale blue starry flowers in late spring and early summer. Despite preferring some moisture, blue star will grow well enough in more general garden conditions, and will also tolerate some shade, though plants may get leggier.

Amsonia tabernaemontana has a neat, erectly branched habit and will need little or no pruning, although some recommend pruning foliage back by half to a third after flowering, particularly if plants are leggy. This will prevent seeding and new growth will make a bushier, neater plant, greener in summer before the papery leaves turn from light yellow to golden-yellow in autumn.

60–90 cm (2–3 ft) × 45–60 cm (1½–2 ft.)

F late spring to early summer

Z 3–9

Further Recommendations

Apart from its narrower leaves, *A. tabernaemontana* var. *salicifolia* is almost identical to the species, and is the true willow amsonia (a common name often wrongly applied to *A. t.* itself).

Strangely, the smaller *A. orientalis* (syn. *Rhazya orientalis*) which originates from Greece and Turkey is almost identical in flower and leaf to the North American *A. tabernaemontana*, although it is shorter. It too is an easily grown perennial for sun or light shade where not too dry, growing to only 45–60 cm (1½–2 ft.).

→
The compact German introduction *Anaphalis triplinervis* 'Sommerschnee' makes a good frontal group in the Summer Garden at Bressingham in autumn. Late-flowering *Aster ×frikartii* 'Jungfrau' is on the right.

Quite distinct among the blue stars is *Amsonia hubrichtii* which is native to the rockier terrain of Arkansas and Oklahoma. With its willowy stems and light green narrow leaves it makes a feathery bush, to 60–90 cm (2–3 ft.), that moves with the breeze. The spring to early summer flowers are pale blue and held in clusters. Best in full sun, this species receives high marks from garden designers for its foliage en masse, its excellent golden yellow autumn colour, and its ability to tolerate drier soils. **Z** 4–9. Although sometimes slow to establish, the blue stars will be happy in the same spot for years.

Anaphalis triplinervis 'Sommerschnee'

pearly everlasting

A grey-leaved plant that thrives with some moisture and shade, *Anaphalis triplinervis* 'Sommerschnee' is worthy of a greater role.

The species *Anaphalis triplinervis*, the three-veined everlasting, is a spreading but noninvasive clump-forming species native to high altitudes from Afghanistan, through the Himalayas to southwestern China,

found growing in meadows and forest clearings. As a garden plant it is slightly taller than 'Sommerschnee' at 30–45 cm (1–1½ ft.), and attractive not only for its silver-grey woolly stems and leaves, but also for a late summer display of white papery flowers. It is one of very few grey-leaved plants that will grow in moist and even poorly drained soils, and in part shade.

With a more compact, lower-growing and neater habit than the species and white flowers, *Anaphalis triplinervis* 'Sommerschnee' (in English, 'Summersnow') is highly recommended. While adaptable to sun or some shade, 'Sommerschnee' will grow happily in full sun with reasonable drainage in Britain and northwestern North America, where heat is less intense and rainfall more regular, but in regions further south it needs moisture to resist leaf scorch and mildew. For a grey-leaved plant it stands up well to humidity. Plants will spread slowly and after a few years, once they have formed a mat of foliage, they are

→
The bright silvery leaves of *Artemisia ludoviciana* 'Valerie Finnis', shown here in early summer, hardly need flowers to create contrasts with a wide range of other plants.

best divided in spring and replanted. The flowers, which continue for weeks, form tight clusters on 20–30-cm (8–12-in.) stems and, for cutting, should be picked just before opening. Spent flowers can be deadheaded but the main cut back should be left until spring.

20–30 cm (8–12 in.) × 45–60 cm (1½–2 ft.)

F late summer to autumn

Z 3–8

Further Recommendations
Much more vigorous is *A. margaritacea*, native to northern North America and northeastern Asia and naturalized in central Europe. It grows in drier, often more open situations in hills or mountain regions on slopes and hillsides and in forest clearings. The dark grey-green leaves are silvery white and woolly beneath, and erect stems bear clusters of pearly white papery flowers. It is more versatile than *A. triplinervis* in being more amenable to sun and dry situations, but it is also prone to being invasive. Height will vary depending on soil and moisture. 60–90 cm (2–3 ft.) × 60–75 cm (2–2½ ft.), F late summer to autumn, **Z** 3–8.

Artemisia ludoviciana 'Valerie Finnis'

western mugwort, white sage

Despite a colonizing habit, this is one of the showiest and toughest silver-leaved perennials and an excellent foil to other plants.

Although naturalized over much of North America, the species *A. ludoviciana* is native from the Midwest prairies to the Pacific coast, from British Columbia in the north down to Mexico. Growing mostly in dry open ground or light woodland, it is silver- or grey-leaved with a vigorous spreading habit, the insignificant small, white or creamy-yellow flowers appearing in late summer on 60–90-cm (2–3-ft.) stems.

→
The glossy evergreen leaves of the carpet-forming wild ginger, *Asarum europaeum*, make a pleasing foil to the fern, *Athyrium niponicum* var. *pictum*, and the spotted leaves of a pulmonaria.

A. ludoviciana 'Valerie Finnis' is a selection spotted by enthusiastic English plantswoman Valerie Finnis, who took it to Beth Chatto's nursery for trial. It was Beth who gave it Valerie's name—a nice story for a distinctive plant whose main feature is its bright silver, willowy leaves, some of which are broader and jaggedly lobed. The flower stems are generally shorter than those of the species, and the small silvery grey flowers are appreciated by flower-arrangers.

A. l. 'Valerie Finnis' grows best in full sun with good drainage, but will happily tolerate some light shade. The silver-white foliage can be prone to rot or mildew in high temperatures and humid conditions, but trimming foliage back in late summer should produce a carpet of silver by autumn. Even in the driest soils, 'Valerie Finnis' and others of the species are invasive, not deep-rooted—so can be controlled by removing runners on an annual basis. For more cautious gardeners, retaining bricks, paving or hidden polythene 10–15 cm (4–6 in.) deep prior to planting is an option when planting among perennials, although the spreading habit can be an advantage if planting for ground cover around a purple-leaved shrub such as *Cotinus* or *Physocarpus*. Since flowers can be floppy, you may choose to prune emerging flower stems by a third or a half in late spring, and again later in summer, creating a stronger and neater foliage effect.

60–75 cm (2–2½ ft.) × 60–75 cm (2–2½ ft.), spreading
F mid to late summer
Z 4–8

Further Recommendations

The popular *A. ludoviciana* 'Silver Queen' is equally robust, yet has perhaps less impressive foliage than 'Valerie Finnis'. With cream to yellow flowers, it reaches 75–90 cm (2½–3 ft.). **Z** 4–8.

Asarum europaeum

hardy ginger, wild ginger

A lowly, extremely useful, noninvasive ground cover plant with glossy green leaves, *Asarum europaeum* has year-round appeal.

The evergreen European wild ginger, with deep glossy green kidney-shaped leaves, is found in moist, shady woodland from western France across to Russia and Siberia. Although popular and sold widely as ground cover on both sides of the Atlantic, it is still little known or yet appreciated by

→
One of the best and most reliable autumn-flowering asters, *Aster* 'Little Carlow', makes a vivid contrast to *Rhus typhina* 'Dissecta' in Foggy Bottom.

leaved hostas can emerge. You will need to look beneath the leaves in spring to observe the curiously shaped purple-brown flowers, and if you crush the roots or leaves you will detect the aroma of ginger; the plant has many herbal properties.

Asarum europaeum traditionally does best in shade or half shade with some moisture in the soil, but at Foggy Bottom it grows well, if not spreading widely, on dry soils in deep shade where few other plants thrive. When first planting, ensure adequate moisture with good drainage. Once established, plants can be divided in spring or early autumn and planted, but not too deeply. In midwinter a carpet of glossy green foliage is to be cherished, perhaps with a clump of snowdrops emerging through it. Despite being very hardy, *A. europaeum* dislikes the heat and humidity of the southeastern United States. (Conversely, many of the strikingly leaved North American wild gingers sulk in the cooler northern European climates.)
15–20 cm (6–8 in.) × 15–30 cm (6–12 in.)
F spring
Z 4–7

gardeners. It is a plant that grows on you, as you observe how it spreads to form a mat of foliage from which plants such as golden- or variegated-

Aster 'Little Carlow'

I would not be without *A.* 'Little Carlow'. Easy and trouble-free, it provides an essential blue to complement autumnal leaf colours.

The main parent of this outstanding perennial is the blue wood aster, *Aster cordifolius*, a variable species that tolerates cold, heat and some shade, native to North America from Nova Scotia in Canada to the southern states of Georgia and Alabama. Its puzzling name was given by Mrs. Thornley, a breeder of asters from Devizes, Wiltshire in England in the 1930s and '40s, who crossed it with mildew-prone *A. novi-belgii*.

It has taken many years for *A.* 'Little Carlow' to be recognized as a great garden plant and cut flower. It

It is *Aster* time at the Picton Garden at Old Court Nurseries (near Malvern, Worcestershire, in England), famous for their *Aster* breeding and a British National Collection holding of this important group of perennials. In this walled-in prairie-style planting, *Aster novae-angliae* 'Lye End Beauty' is planted in front of *Rudbeckia tomentosa*, which in turn makes a striking contrast with the purple *A. n.-a.* 'Colwall Constellation', the taller *Eupatorium maculatum* 'Purpureum' adding perspective on the left with other asters in the background.

is a vigorous but not spreading plant, with rich green leaves and dark green arching well-branched 120-cm (4-ft.) stems that are festooned with a mass of small lavender-blue yellow-centred flowers in late summer, deepening to a vibrant violet-blue into autumn. While tolerating light shade, *A.* 'Little Carlow' is best in full sun on well-drained but moisture-retentive soil. On heavier or moister soils stems it may get tall and flop after heavy summer rains, so an early summer pruning-back by a third to half will create a bushier if slightly later-flowering plant. This is a trouble-free perennial, though occasionally prone to mildew. It may benefit from replanting every few years if the rootstock becomes woody and overcrowded.
120 cm (4 ft.) × 60–75 cm (2–2½ ft.)
F late summer to autumn
Z 3–9

Further Recommendations
The following recommendations include a selection of late-flowering, trouble-free cultivars. (Earlier-flowering asters are listed under *A.* ×*frikartii* 'Monch'.)

A. ×*herveyi* may be little known following its recent name change; it was formerly *A. macrophyllus* 'Twilight'. Under either name, it goes up in my estimation every year. From broad mounds of dark green oval leaves, it puts up 90–120-cm (3–4-ft.) free-standing stems with branched heads of bright lilac-blue flowers that continue for weeks. Beyond a long flowering performance from late summer well into autumn, it seems to perform well in quite dry positions in shade.

The North American aromatic aster, *A. oblongifolius*, with fragrant foliage, is little known in Europe, but in *A. o.* 'Raydon's Favorite', 120 cm (4 ft.) high, and *A. o.* 'October Skies', 90 cm (3 ft.) high, we have two excellent bushy violet-blue, broad spreading autumn asters, needing full sun or light shade, with good winter drainage. Cut back both by half in early summer for a more compact habit.

A. ericoides, originating from an area in North America similar to that of *A. cordifolius*, and its cultivars are tolerant of heat and dry soils, providing grace and colour in the autumn garden. Cultivars of note are *A. e.* 'Brimstone', yellow in bud, opening to white, and *A. e.* 'Pink Cloud', pale pink, both 90 cm (3 ft.) high, as well as the more upright *A. e.* 'White Heather', reaching 120 cm (4 ft.), with dainty white flowers.

For real knockout colour, few asters can beat the German selection of the New England aster, *A. novae-angliae* 'Andenken an Alma Potschke' (are we really expected to repeat that every time we mention the plant?). It makes a sturdy, relatively compact bush of stiff, upright, well-branched stems covered in glowing scarlet-pink flowers from late summer to autumn, drawing the eye to its stunning, if hardly natural-looking, display. Once again, prune back in early summer for a shorter plant, normally growing to 120–150 cm (4–5 ft.).

The last and the smallest aster I recommend, *A. lateriflorus* 'Prince', 30–45 cm (1–1½ ft.) high, has fairly insignificant autumn flowers, but should mainly be grown for its striking purple-bronze foliage that makes a show from early spring onwards, toning down in sun and useful for so many plant association, or for edging a pathway. The purple-bronze stems and small pink and white flowers make a good late show, but need a light background to enhance them. All **Z** 3–8.

Aster ×frikartii 'Monch'

Long-flowering and graceful with beautifully rayed lavender-blue petals, this aster is a gardener's delight.

I worked at the Frikart nursery in Stafa, near Zurich, Switzerland in 1961, little realizing what contribution they had made to the horticultural world with their introductions around 1920 of three asters which are now world famous. These were crosses between *Aster amellus*, the Italian starwort, and *Aster thomsonii*, a species from the Himalayas. Karl Frikart named them for the famous Bernese Oberland mountains, Eiger, Monch and Jungfrau. The others are still grown and appreciated, but *A. ×f.* 'Monch' has become the icon of asters and deservedly so, even though it needs careful handling to make the most of its attributes.

It forms a slowly developing clump with many slender, multi-branched stems to 90 cm (3 ft.), and in late mid-summer until early autumn frosts it produces a succession of soft lavender-blue yellow-centred flowers as wide as 8 cm (3 in.) across. Best not overcrowded by other plants, it is mildew-free and will grow in sun or light shade, and once established it will continue for years as long as it has good winter drainage. That said, there is a limit to its cold and heat tolerance, as designated in hardiness zones 5–8, and unfortunately for gardeners they are seen as unreliably perennial in the southern United States. *A. ×f.* 'Monch' is best planted in spring as undeveloped roots in autumn can lack substance and succumb to winter wet. (This same advice applies to other *A. ×frikartii* hybrids and to *Aster amellus*.)
75–90 cm (2½–3 ft.) × 60–75 cm (2–2½ ft.)
F mid to late summer
Z 5–8

Further Recommendations
A. ×frikartii 'Wunder von Stäfa', introduced in 1924, is often confused with *A. ×f.* 'Monch' although it is shorter and more lax in habit. I rate *A. ×f.* 'Jungfrau' for its upright, bushier form, 60–75 cm (2–2½ ft.) high, and mass of deep violet-blue flowers late into autumn, as well as the diminutive *A. ×frikartii* 'Flora's Delight', 30–45 cm (1–1½ ft.) tall, named after my stepmother Flora Bloom. Given good winter drainage, 'Flora's Delight' can be reliably perennial, with a flowering performance to match or exceed that of *A. ×f.* 'Monch'.

It has probably become clear that my favourite asters are in shades of blue—a colour so valuable in the later summer and autumn garden. Few asters make such a dramatic impact as *A. amellus* 'Veilchenkönigin', translated as 'Violet Queen'. It was raised by the legendary Karl Foerster in Potsdam, Germany in 1966 (while behind the Iron Curtain), and makes a long-flowering display, 30–45 cm (1–1½

In a semi-shady position in the Summer Garden at Bressingham, three plants of *Aster ×trikartii* 'Monch' hold up well on their own, flowering for weeks from late summer.

→

Astilbe chinensis var. *taquetii* 'Superba' is one of the most imposing astilbes, showing erect plumed heads of magenta-purple flowers on 120-cm (4-ft.) stems in late summer.

ft.) high, with a mass of vibrant violet flowers until autumn frosts. No other cultivar within this species makes such an impact. Plant in spring in well-drained soil and do not overcrowd with vigorous neighbours. **Z** 5–8.

Astilbe chinensis var. taquetii 'Superba'

false spiraea

Although less spectacular in colour than some astilbes, for reliability, longevity, foliage and late flower *A. c.* var. *taquetii* 'Superba' is indeed superb.

There are well over 200 cultivars of moisture-loving astilbes, formerly listed under the name *Spiraea* and commonly called the false spiraea. Most of these species are native to eastern Asia and one, *A. biternata*, to North America. Since their introduction to gardens in the 19th century a considerable amount of hybridizing between species and cultivars has resulted in a wide range of types and colours, with heights of pretty plumed flowers ranging from 10 cm (4 in.) to 180 cm (6 ft.). Most require some shade and all require moisture, although *A. chinensis* and its forms are more tolerant of drier soils in cooler climates if only for temporary periods. They are excellent at the waterside, but do not like being waterlogged, particularly in summer.

Like the species *A. chinensis* which originates from damp meadows, woodland and streamsides in Russia, China and Korea, *Astilbe chinensis* var. *taquetii* 'Superba' has a spreading habit, making a carpet of glossy green leaves and a fine show of magenta-purple flowers on erect 120–150-cm (4–5-ft.) stems in late summer. Many astilbe flowerheads remain attractive in winter, so unless seeding is a problem, delay cutting until spring. All astilbes prefer moist humus-rich soils. Older plants can become woody and should be divided every few years, keeping the younger material; firm in when replanting, and mulch with leaf mould or composted pine bark.
120–150 cm (4–5 ft.) × 60–90 cm (2–3 ft.)
F mid to late summer
Z 4–8

→

An early summer close-up view of *Astrantia major* 'Ruby Wedding' shows clusters of tiny flowers surrounded by ruby-red bracts resembling petals. Like all astrantias, it makes an excellent cut flower.

Further Recommendations

For an almost more spectacular show than that of 'Superba', *A. c.* var. *t.* 'Purpurlanze' ('Purple Lance'), similar but taller, grows on rich soils to 180 cm (6 ft.) and is a glowing purplish red. At the other end of the scale, again more tolerant of drier conditions, are *A. chinensis* 'Pumila', a good ground cover at a pathway's edge with tight sprays of lilac-purple from 30 to 45 cm (1–1½ ft.) tall, and the startlingly bright purple *A. c.* 'Visions' at a similar height, a vigorous plant with glossy green leaves flowering in midsummer. Both **Z** 4–8.

For colour, and to recognize that great astilbe breeder Georg Arends who bred them and many others, choose the striking crimson-red, slender spiked *A.* ×*arendsii* 'Fanal', introduced in 1933, and the brilliant creamy white *A.* ×*arendsii* 'Brautschleier' ('Bridal Veil'), introduced in 1929; both are 60 cm (2 ft.) high. For grace and beauty of form select the arching sprays of the pink *A.* 'Straussenfeder' ('Ostrich Plume') or the white of *A. t.* 'Professor van der Wielen', introduced in 1917. Both reach 120 cm (4 ft.) in height and as much across, flowering midsummer.

Lastly, for foliage and flower in the smaller garden or patio containers, consider the Alan Bloom selection: *A. simplicifolia* 'Sprite', which forms a compact 15–20-cm (6–8-in.) mound of deep bronze-green finely cut foliage followed by delicate 30-cm (1-ft.) sprays of pearl-pink flowers for weeks in mid to late summer. All **Z** 4–8.

Astrantia major 'Ruby Wedding'

masterwort

In midsummer 'Ruby Wedding' creates a stunning display of deep ruby-red bracts and long-lasting flowers.

A. major, the greater masterwort, is native to moist alpine meadows in mountainous areas from northwest Spain across the Pyrenees and Alps as far as eastern Russia. It is best with moisture and part shade, but happy enough in cooler climates in full sun. The species is variable in the wild, and forms vigorous leafy spreading clumps with a central head of near-white flowers held above a circle of petals or papery bracts, excellent for cutting or drying. Much breeding and selection in recent years, mostly among this species, has given us a wonderful choice of attractive summer-flowering perennials.

Despite being among the oldest of more recent selections, *A. m.* 'Ruby Wedding' is perhaps still the best of an increasing range, with deep red or maroon flowers and bracts, glowing intensely when touched by morning or evening light. All are prone to self-seeding, so according to choice, the old flowerheads can be enjoyed and resulting seedlings selected for growing on, or spent flowers should be deadheaded regularly. If plants are to be kept true, division of named cultivars should be made in spring.
45–60 cm (1½–2 ft.) × 30–45 cm (1–1½ ft.)
F early to late summer
Z 4–7

→
Fresh green pea-like foliage shows off the rich blue flowers of long-lived, reliable *Baptisia australis* in early summer in the Dell Garden.

Further Recommendations

Two other selections of *Astrantia major* should be mentioned: *A. m.* 'Roma', a deep rosy pink selected by garden designer Piet Oudolf; and *A. m.* 'Sunningdale Variegated', in spring one of the most striking of perennials with cream-and-white splashed leaves, which turn green followed by white, pink-flushed flowers. Both 60–75 cm (2–2½ ft.), **Z** 4–7. Astrantias do not tolerate prolonged heat and humidity, so are unlikely to be successful in many southern and midwestern American states, although keen gardeners may want to try anyway.

Baptisia australis

blue false indigo

For longevity, foliage and flower this easy perennial is worthy of much wider recognition.

The slowly spreading *Baptisia australis* clumps in the Dell Garden at Bressingham have given a show without disturbance for more than 30 years. Any plant that is so reliable, showy and trouble-free merits inclusion in this book. Native to the western Appalachians across the midwestern plains to Kansas, down to Georgia and Texas, this is a handsome but variable species, tolerant of heat and drought once established. It forms a shrubby bush of upright stems clothed in blue-green leaves, in fertile soils reaching as high as 180 cm (6 ft.). The lupin-like flowers can vary from rich blue through lilac blue to violet, making a show for a few weeks in summer, maintaining interest as swollen seedpods develop, turning black and still held on spikes as autumn frosts clear the leaves.

In the wild, *Baptisia australis* grows in woods, sandy floodplains and river banks, but in gardens it is best to give full sun and good drainage; too fertile or part shade and plants will flop. Pruning a third of new growth away with shears to a mound immediately after flowering will prevent this and create a leafier foliage plant, but of course there will be no seedpods to follow. Cut back foliage in winter, and remember that new growth appears only in late spring.
120–180 cm (4–6 ft.) × 60–90 cm (2–3 ft.)
F early summer
Z 4–8

Further Recommendations

Baptisia 'Purple Smoke' is a chance hybrid between *B. australis* and *B. alba* with striking charcoal-grey stems and purple flowers in summer. It is vigorous, so allow space for its development. Place in full sun, so that its glaucous summer foliage can contrast with other later-flowering North American natives such as heleniums, heliopsis or rudbeckias. 90–150 cm (3–5 ft.) × 90–120 cm (3–4 ft.), **Z** 4–8. For a yellow, look for the early summer flowering *Baptisia* 'Carolina Moonlight' a hybrid of *B. sphaerocarpa* and *B. alba*, with more dainty spikes of pale yellow pea-like flowers and blue-green foliage. 90–120 cm (3–4 ft.) × 60–90 cm (2–3 ft.), flowers early summer, **Z** 4–8. Both 'Purple Smoke' and 'Carolina Moonlight' were discovered by Rob Gardener of the North Carolina Botanical Garden.

←

A midwinter shot after an early morning frost shows the depth of colour on the leathery leaves of *Bergenia* 'Bressingham Ruby', as captured in the watery sunlight in the Winter Garden, Bressingham.

Bergenia 'Bressingham Ruby'

elephant's ears

A truly year-round plant, *Bergenia* 'Bressingham Ruby' changes with the seasons, saving its most spectacular show for winter.

Much breeding work over many years, from the original seven or eight species of *Bergenia* that mostly originate from central or eastern Asia, have today given gardeners an excellent choice of foliage and flowering perennials. Bergenias are mostly clump forming plants with evergreen, leathery-looking largely rounded leaves, and in spring emerging spikes carry many pendulous goblet-shaped flowers from white through pink to crimson. What has led to them being such useful and popular plants is the ability of certain species and selected cultivars to change leaf colour from green in summer to purple, crimson or ruby in winter. Having tried many of these, it is nice to know that *B.* 'Bressingham Ruby', a selection we raised at Bressingham and introduced in 1984, is among the best (and of course, for me, *the* best).

It forms a neat, compact plant with bright glossy green leaves in summer,

gradually deepening to ruby red with crimson-purple undersides into winter, the colour more intense when plants are under stress and in full sun. In spring new growth and old leaves turn back to green as deep pink flowers make a show on 60-cm (2-ft.) spikes, although (like all bergenias) these can be damaged by spring frosts. *B.* 'Bressingham Ruby' will grow in all but the wettest or driest soil and will thrive, but not colour so well, in shade where not too dry. Older clumps can be pulled apart and replanted in early autumn or after flowering in spring. Cut away dead or disfigured leaves at any time. In colder regions where no snow cover exists, prolonged drying or freezing winds can damage foliage. Covering with evergreen trimmings will help to protect the plants during these periods.
30–45 cm (1–1½ ft.) × 30–45 cm (1–1½ ft.)
F spring
Z 4–8

Further Recommendations
B. 'Eric Smith', *B.* 'Rotblum' and *B. cordifolia* 'Winterglut' are other good winter colour cultivars. Two reliable white-flowered cultivars should also

be recommended; although neither has attractive winter foliage, the two share a history. *Bergenia* 'Silberlicht' ('Silver Light') was selected by renowned German nurseryman Georg Arends over 50 years ago, and my father Alan Bloom and Percy Piper raised seedlings from Arends's plant to introduce *B.* 'Bressingham White' in 1976. Both have Awards of Garden Merit from the Royal Horticultural Society, but *B.* 'Bressingham White' arguably has a more attractive foliage and habit and clearer white flowers, though both varieties fade to pink with age. Both are 45–60 cm (1½–2 ft.) × 60–75 cm (2–2½ ft.), flowering in spring. **Z** 4–8. Georg Arends also raised the remarkable *B.* 'Morgenrote' (*B.* 'Morning Red') which forms a handsome, large-leaved plant, excellent for ground cover, with carmine pink flowers on 45–60-cm (1½–2-ft.) spikes in spring and again in late summer. **Z** 4–8.

←

You can feel spring is about to burst forth as the first flowers and silver marbled leaves of *Brunnera macrophylla* 'Jack Frost' emerge in spring, highlighted by the crimson flowers of *Bergenia* 'Eroica' behind in this combination at Foggy Bottom.

→

From early spring, the pink-flushed variegated leaves of *Calamagrostis ×acutiflora* 'Overdam' have been an attraction—and now, in early summer, pinkish inflorescences catch the morning sun in Foggy Bottom, with *Kniphofia* 'Shining Sceptre' providing contrasting colour.

Brunnera macrophylla 'Jack Frost'

With bright blue forget-me-not flowers in spring and silver marbled leaves all summer, *B.* 'Jack Frost' is a joy.

The species *Brunnera macrophylla* is a native to northeastern Turkey, the Caucasus and Georgia to western Siberia in forests and open grassy slopes, forming a compact clump with bright blue forget-me-not flowers on wispy branchlets in early spring, followed by coarse heart-shaped leaves that remain to make good ground cover all summer. The species and some cultivars will grow in full sun in cooler summer regions. *B.* 'Jack Frost' is a relatively new introduction that arose as a mutation or sport in the micropropagation unit at Walters Gardens in Michigan, and has already found a place as one of my favourite gardenworthy plants: hardy, reliable and undeniably showy.

'Jack Frost' makes a fine and long spring display of light twinkling blue flowers, but it is the silver-veined and marbled leaves that follow that make it a valuable plant for garden and container. As its origins suggest, 'Jack Frost' is very hardy; however, leaves can be easily scorched in hotter climates in full sun or where dry root conditions exist, so if in any doubt plant in full or part shade where roots are moist. Old flowers are best removed as soon as flowering is finished, and if the foliage becomes damaged during summer cut back, water and mulch for another show of brighter, cleaner leaves, although these may be smaller. This plant offers so many opportunities for plant combinations throughout its season from spring to autumn: try it with the black-leaved *Ophiopogon planiscapus* 'Nigrescens'. Propagation is by division, but damaged roots may regrow with green leaves so care should be taken. 'Jack Frost' and other selections will seed freely on moist soils if flowers are not removed, but will vary from the parent.
45–60 cm (1½–2 ft.) × 60 cm (2 ft.)
F spring
Z 3–8

Further Recommendations

Brunnera macrophylla 'Hadspen Cream' was raised by English plantsman Eric Smith and is a robust alternative to *B.* 'Jack Frost', with mid-green heart-shaped leaves edged irregularly with creamy yellow. It is free flowering and makes good, dense ground cover once established in part shade. 30–45 cm (1–1½ ft.) × 45–60cm (1½–2 ft.), **F** spring, **Z** 3–8.

Calamagrostis ×acutiflora 'Overdam'

variegated feather reed grass

This attractive ornamental grass displays changing foliage and flower from spring until winter.

C. ×acutiflora arose as a natural hybrid between two Eurasian species, *C. epigios* and *C. arundinacea*, both native to open woodlands and moist meadows. What is now considered the original hybrid was named many years ago by renowned German plantsman Karl Foerster as *C. ×acutiflora* 'Stricta'. After his death, nomenclatural rules changed, disallowing this name—so, fittingly, *C. ×a.* 'Stricta' became *C. ×a.* 'Karl Foerster'. This is a vigorous and

→
The large, well-branched spikes of violet-blue flowers on *Campanula lactiflora* 'Prichard's Variety' are an important ingredient in the summer perennial garden.

widely used clump-forming plant with early glossy green leaves somewhat lax in habit, followed by slender but strongly erect stems to 180 cm (6 ft.) with purple-tinged flowers in summer. These closely held flowers, followed by leaves, turn beige in autumn, remaining attractive into winter.

Why am I describing C. ×a. 'Karl Foerster' when my selection is C. ×a. 'Overdam'? Well, in this case the two are similar and equally outstanding, but 'Overdam' is particularly recommended for its great spring appeal, with early pink-tinged leaves striped white and cream. Depending on conditions, the foliage will reach just 60–90 cm (2–3 ft.), brightly variegated in early summer, turning greener as the season progresses. The narrow, erect stems of both have an architectural quality that persists well into winter, making C. ×a. 'Karl Foerster' in particular a popular landscape plant.

Both add movement and grace during windy conditions, seldom lying down for long after inclement weather. Cut back foliage in late winter to 15 cm (6 in.) to prepare for the new season. Both are best in full sun where not too dry, growing well even on heavy clay soils. Divide and plant before new growth begins in early spring. Mainly trouble free, but leaves can show rust in constant wet or overly humid conditions in summer, or where plants are congested.

90–120 cm (3–4 ft.) × 30–45 cm (1–1½ ft.)
F summer into autumn
Z 4–8

Campanula lactiflora 'Prichard's Variety'

milky bellflower

Not always readily available, *C. l.* 'Prichard's Variety' is yet to become widely appreciated for what it can contribute to the summer garden.

There are innumerable species and cultivars of the bellflower, but some are invasive, some temperamental and some short-lived. Some are undoubtedly beautiful but difficult to please;

showy *Campanula lactiflora*, the milky bellflower, is more reliable. Native to the Caucasus to western Asia, it grows in forest clearings and alpine meadows, but so freely does it seed that it has become naturalized in other countries where it has been introduced. It makes a fleshy thong-rooted clump, roots and stems exuding a milky sap when cut or damaged. The species and seedlings will vary from 60 to 180 cm (2–6 ft.) in height, with rather coarse, hairy leaves and flower spikes bearing clusters of open bell-shaped flowers in midsummer.

The plants can be very long lived given good deep soil that is not too dry in sun or part shade, but spent heads should be cut as soon as flowering has finished, as self-seeded plants that follow the next year will vary considerably. In moist soils plants may get tall and stems may flop later in the season. In this case, shear back emerging stems

In early summer *Campanula poscharskyana* 'Blue Waterfall' makes an eye catching splash as it hangs over a flint wall at Foggy Bottom.

→

With its grassy mounded form and its bronzed leaves, *Carex comans* 'Bronze Form' is an excellent foil to golden *Anthemis tinctoria* and blue *Geranium* flowers in summer.

by one third in spring and you will get more flowers (appearing a bit later). *C. l.* 'Prichard's Variety' was raised by and named for the Prichard nursery of Christchurch before 1950.

90 × 120 cm (3–4 ft.) × 75–90 cm (2½–3 ft.)

F early midsummer

Z 5–8

Further Recommendations

The slightly larger-flowered *C. l.* 'Superba' is equally good. There are also white forms in the tall *C. l.* 'Alba' and *C. l.* 'Avalanche', and a light blue in the 120-cm (4-ft) *C. l.* 'Blue Cross'. The almost-diminutive *C. l.* 'Pouffe', raised and named by Alan Bloom, makes a 30–45-cm (1–1½-ft.) mound of light green leaves covered in pale blue flowers. I suspect one of the reasons for these campanulas not being more widely grown is that they do not present well in containers at garden centres.

For versatility and performance, the Serbian bellflower, *C. poscharskyana*, takes some beating, although it may not perform so well in areas with high summer heat and humidity. Nevertheless where its cultivars can be grown they are deciduous or semi-evergreen,

forming mounds of bright green toothed leaves with a mass of star-shaped flowers on tendril-like stems in early summer. These are good edging plants, for sun or part shade, ideal for growing over a wall or beneath roses or shrubs where not too dry. I confess an interest, having selected several distinct forms from seedlings raised at Foggy Bottom, the first and most widely distributed named 'Blue Waterfall'. This makes a compact clump, whose flowering stems spread widely, covered in clear blue flowers that are repeated if cut back later in summer. In cooler seasons or climates, plants will flower all summer and autumn in hanging baskets or pots, and continue through winter if brought into a cool glasshouse or conservatory. 20–30 cm (8–12 in.) × 60–75 cm (2–2½ ft.), flowering early summer to late autumn, **Z** 4–8.

Carex comans 'Bronze Form'

New Zealand hairy sedge

One of the most striking of New Zealand sedges, *Carex comans* 'Bronze Form' is indispensable for creating form and colour in the year

round garden (despite its reputation for sometimes looking dead).

There are well over a thousand sedges. These grass-like plants grow mostly in damp situations in various parts of the world, but the majority are from temperate or arctic regions. Some are extremely ornamental, more appreciated for their foliage than for their inflorescences or flower; for the garden, many of the most useful are the evergreen clump-forming species and cultivars from New Zealand.

Carex comans 'Bronze Form' is a particularly striking selection from the hairy sedge, *C. comans*, which is native to both North and South Islands of New Zealand where it grows in moist, open areas and forest clearings. From a central clump it makes a wide spreading tussock of narrow reddish bronze leaves, shorter stems bearing small, brown, insignificant flowers, some leaves curled and wispy at the ends. In the moist conditions it prefers, 'Bronze Form' seeds freely and almost true to type, which is useful for replacing older plants. Best in full sun or light shade, it will tolerate some summer drought if not combined with excessive prolonged heat.

Valuable for its year-round appeal,

C. c. 'Bronze Form' contrasts well with other plants, and with mulch such as stone or gravel. Older plants retain dead leaves; comb these out by hand in early spring, using gloves as leaves can be abrasive, trimming perhaps a third of the remaining leaves to tidy up for the new season. Older clumps can be divided and replanted, and older or dead material discarded. 30–45 cm (1–1½ in.) × 60–75 cm (2–2½ ft.)
F spring to early summer
Z 7–8

Further Recommendations

Not surprisingly, there are other selections in this species, and New Zealand plantsman Terry Hatch spotted one growing at Cape Egmont, North Island with light grey-green leaves ageing to silver white, and appropriately called it *C. c.* 'Frosted Curls'. It offers a striking contrast to the black-leaved *Ophiopogon planiscapus* 'Nigrescens' and other colourful flow-ers or foliage. It is similar in habit to *C. c.* 'Bronze Form' but perhaps a little less vigorous. Like all of the New Zealand sedges, it may suffer winter loss in poorly drained conditions.

C. flagillifera, the mop-headed sedge, is often confused with *C. c.* 'Bronze Form'; it is lighter-coloured, with leaves that are rougher to the touch and it spreads more widely along the ground, but is equally useful and excellent in containers. *Carex buchananii*, the leatherleaf sedge, is also similar in colour to 'Bronze Form' but has a distinctly erect habit to 60 cm (2 ft.), the leaves wispy and curled at the tips. *Carex tenuiculmis*, similar in habit and size to 'Bronze Form', is one of my favourites for its almost metallic sheen on dark bronze-brown leaves. All **Z** 7.

I make no apologies for this extended list of recommended sedges as they are such valuable year-round-interest plants. *Carex oshimensis* 'Evergold' is a sport from the compact, tough, hardy green-leaved Japanese sedge that grows in drier conditions than the New Zealand sedges. Its rich glossy green leaves make good ground cover, but *C. o.* 'Evergold' is brightness itself all year, with creamy white to yellow leaves edged green, excellent for edging pathways or for patio containers. Flowers are insignificant. Plant in sun or shade. 30–45 cm (1–1½ ft.) × 45–60 cm (1½–2 ft.), **F** spring to early summer, **Z** 5–8.

Long-lived and useful for a wide range of conditions is the tufted sedge, *Carex elata* 'Aurea'. Native to northern Europe, the green-leaved species grows well in moist conditions, even beside water, and can also thrive in drier soils although it will scorch under very hot, dry conditions. *C. e.* 'Aurea' has golden leaves edged with green, particularly bright in spring and early summer, and spikes of brown heads with yellow stamens on male flowers. 60–75 cm (2–2½ ft.) × 60 cm (2 ft.), **F** spring to early summer, **Z** 5–8.

An imposing ten-year-old clump of the New Zealand native *Chionochloa rubra* flowers in the Foggy Bottom garden in late summer.

→

Autumn colours are reflected in the warm-toned flowers of hardy *Chrysanthemum* 'Apricot' in the Dell Garden. *Persicaria amplexicaulis* 'Firetail' is behind.

Chionochloa rubra

red tussock grass

Wherever this impressive New Zealand evergreen grass can be grown, it adds dramatic year-round presence. Having grown it at Bressingham for many years, I find it invaluable for its stature and movement among other grasses and perennials. It resembles a giant version of *Carex comans*, forming a large tussock of coppery bronze foliage over two to three years, with leaves arching gracefully from a central clump, catching every breeze. In drier soils leaves may have a more faded appearance, since this species, widespread in open areas on North and South Islands of New Zealand, prefers moist conditions (although it will tolerate drought). Small, insignificant flowers appear on stems among the foliage, but this is also a foliage plant to grow as a specimen or in a container—eventually a rather large one. Plants can be divided with difficulty in spring, discarding old material, not allowing roots to dry out before replanting, and keeping them well watered. They can be raised from seed if not readily available from local garden centres.
90–120 cm (3–4 ft.) × 90–120 cm (3–4 ft.)
F spring to early summer
Z 8

Chrysanthemum 'Apricot'

The showy and truly hardy perennial chrysanthemums, of which 'Apricot' is a strong example, add a vital colour ingredient to the autumn garden.

Chrysanthemums, which for a short period of confusion went under the name *Dendranthema*, include the highly bred cut flower and pot Mums, the majority of which are neither hardy nor suitable for gardens. This should not prevent a full appreciation of those that are perfectly good perennials in both single- and double-flowered forms. Many of those considered in the Rubellum Group have been around for many years and have a spreading habit and mostly single flowers. 'Apricot' has 6-cm (2½-in.) wide flat-headed flowers with sparkling apricot-pink petals and golden yellow centres. Like other *Chrysanthemum* cultivars it is easily grown, and best in full sun in most soils where neither too wet nor too dry.
60–90 cm (2–3 ft.) × 60–90 cm (2–3 ft.)
F autumn
Z 5–9

Further Recommendations
Popular in the United States is the similar but more compact 'Hillside Sheffield', found in a garden in Sheffield, Connecticut by Fred McGourty of Hillside Gardens in the same state. Some of the still-outstanding garden cultivars date back to the 1930s when English breeder and nurseryman Reginald Perry introduced the rose-pink 'Clara Curtis' with 6-cm (2½-in.) wide flowers, 60 cm (2 ft.) tall, followed in 1942 by the smaller 5-cm (2-in.) wide, soft apricot-yellow 'Mary Stoker', 75 cm (2½ ft.) tall, and in 1948 with the striking deep-crimson-red semi-double 'Duchess of Edinburgh'.

With most *Chrysanthemum* cultivars, including 'Apricot', it pays to shear the top 10–15 cm (4–6 in.) of new growth in mid spring and

←
In late summer, sunshine-coloured flowers and fine filigree foliage on the indispensable *Coreopsis verticillata* 'Zagreb' make a bright contrast to the shasta daisy, *Leucanthemum maximum*, behind, in the Summer Garden at Bressingham.

Coreopsis verticillata 'Zagreb'

threadleaf coreopsis

Among the threadleaf coreopsis, 'Zagreb' wins my vote as one of the best and toughest performers suitable for a sunny position in any garden.

In the wild, *Coreopsis verticillata* grows in open woods, meadows and dry areas from Maryland in the north, south to Florida and east to Kansas, where it reaches 60–90 cm (2–3 ft.). The species and cultivars have mid-green slender leaves and bright yellow daisy-like flowers for many weeks in summer, and have a spreading rather than invasive habit, although this may depend on conditions. They are sun-lovers and tolerate extreme heat and drought, but are also amenable to cooler climates and a wide range of soils. *C. v.* 'Zagreb', whose origin is a mystery (at least to me), is the lowest growing of the cultivars, providing a mass of bright golden yellow blooms in mid to late summer. With 'Zagreb' and other cultivars, if flowering is sporadic by late summer and plants look tired, shearing back by half will give a stronger repeat performance in autumn. These are not fussy plants and can be left for a few years before

midsummer to give a greater flowering display, usually occurring in late summer to autumn, depending on cultivar and location. This will also help to prevent stems from flopping later in the season. The trimming or pinching is of course a personal choice, and may only apply to taller cultivars. It is best to leave the woody stems over winter and prune back in spring. Older plants can be lifted, divided and replanted in spring every few years. The larger, 7-cm (2¾-in.) flowers are inclined to

flop in moister conditions. There are many more cultivars, but the singles in particular look natural among other perennials and add strikingly beautiful autumnal shades of red, orange, pink and yellow to the hues of an autumn garden. These chrysanthemums are of course excellent for cutting but care should be taken when handling plants and leaves as they can give allergic reactions. Cultivars mentioned are hardy **z** 5–9.

→
Cortaderia selloana 'Pumila' is no ordinary pampas grass: it is just the best for an autumn display of fluffy plumes that last through most of the winter. Seen here with *Cornus sanguinea* 'Midwinter Fire' in the foreground in autumn, in the Winter Garden, Bressingham.

lifting, dividing and replanting in spring to rejuvenate. Being shallow-rooted, any tendency to spread beyond requirement can easily be curbed by a spade as necessary.

25–30 cm (10–12 in.) × 30–45 cm (1–1½ ft.)

F midsummer to early autumn

Z 3–9

Further Recommendations

Also dependable are *C. v.* 'Grandiflora' (syn. *C. v.* 'Golden Shower'), golden yellow and taller at 60 cm (2 ft.) and *C. v.* 'Golden Gain', named at Bressingham, which makes more of a clump-forming habit with deep golden yellow flowers growing to 45–60 cm (1½–2 ft.). All of these are very hardy, but *C. v.* 'Moonbeam', selected by plantsman Bill Archer in England and well named for its dark foliage and contrasting pale lemon yellow flowers, is less reliable: it needs hot summers, and very well-drained soil in winter to remain perennial, but is spectacular where it grows well, perhaps allowing its rather lax habit to adorn a bank. Prune back by half in late spring to create a more compact plant.

Cortaderia selloana 'Pumila'

dwarf pampas grass

Few ornamental grasses can match the magnificent display of the silvery white autumn plumes of 'Pumila', the hardiest of cortaderias.

C. selloana 'Pumila' was selected as a dwarf form of the pampas grass as long ago as 1875, and has consistently been the best performer of the species which is native to Argentina, Chile and Brazil. It slowly develops into a large clump with long arching grey-green sharply serrated leaves, which must be handled with gloves, and in autumn a mass of silvery white, eventually fluffy plumes on 150–180-cm (5–6-ft.) stems, held just above the foliage. The true plant should apparently only reach 120 cm (4 ft.), but such a diminutive stature is seldom seen, and those reaching 180 cm (6 ft.) or shorter will resist winter winds to provide interest (unless in the path of a gale) until early spring.

→
Equally brilliant on its own, *Crocosmia* 'Lucifer' adds to a vibrant combination in the Summer Garden at Bressingham in midsummer, with *Geranium* 'Rozanne' beneath and *Leucanthemum* ×*superbum* 'Becky' behind.

This is the time to cut back old flower stems, tidy up and clean out any congested matter in the centre of the plant. In an open situation where no collateral damage is likely, an annual burning, drastic though it seems, will be the quickest way, even if the initial result is unsightly—and not for the fainthearted, as doing it too late can kill the plant.

The late and mostly bountiful display of plumes gives an element of drama and surprise, but one or more clumps create a stunning focal point where light can shimmer through, and frost adds magic in autumn, plumes of white contrasting with autumnal leaf colours. The plants prefer full sun and light shade, and are happy with most soils; it is worth finding a microclimate in colder regions, although *C. s.* 'Pumila' is considered hardy to **Z** 6. 120–180 cm (4–6 ft.) × 120–150 cm (4–5 ft.)
F autumn into winter
Z 6–9

Crocosmia 'Lucifer'

montbretia

The hardiest and arguably most spectacular of crocosmias, C. 'Lucifer' is worth a place in all but the smallest of gardens.

The seven or so *Crocosmia* species all originate from South Africa, and since the 19th century considerable hybridizing has given us some wonderful selections for adding colour to the summer garden. Strictly speaking they should be classed as bulbs or corms, but the hardier types in particular are looked upon as perennials. Selecting for hardiness was one of my father Alan Bloom's intentions, and while working with Percy Piper in 1963 they crossed the hardiest two species: *C. masoniorum* and *C. paniculata.* Several hundred seedlings arose from this cross, and over the next three years they were assessed and reduced to a final six that were named and introduced in 1966 and then sold in 1970.

All six cultivars have stood the test of time, but 'Lucifer' has become the gardening world's favourite *Crocosmia.* From large clusters of corm-like roots, bright green spear-shaped shoots emerge in spring, quickly form-ing broad, rich, green, ribbed leaves to 120 cm (4 ft.). It is the earliest *Crocosmia* to flower, arching heads of vermillion flame flowers on wiry black-green stems, creating an eyecatching display for several weeks. The combination of foliage, flower and attractive seedheads gives 'Lucifer' great garden value, especially in plant combinations where the flowers are luminescent against the purple foliage of *Cotinus*

coggygria 'Royal Purple' or *Physocarpus opulifolius* 'Diabolo'.

'Lucifer' and other crocosmias need full sun, and even there, given warmth and moisture, the heavy leaves of 'Lucifer' can flop later in summer, so may need some maintenance. In hot summer regions, rust can be a problem, and in both cases discretion should be used in cutting away unsightly foliage. 'Lucifer' and other

crocosmias will grow well enough in any garden soil that is neither too wet nor too dry, but all resent poor drainage in winter. If root growth becomes congested with age, lift in early spring and divide, discard the oldest woody corms, compost the soil and replant. Protect for winter by mulching corms with 10 cm (4 in.) of leaf mould, or alternatively in very cold areas you can also lift the corms in late autumn,

cut off foliage and dry the corms in a frost-free building, and then plant out the next spring. 'Lucifer' cuts such a dash that all this effort is rewarded.
120–150 cm (4–5 ft.) × 60–75 cm (2–2½ ft.)
F mid to late summer
Z 6–9

→
Architectural *Cynara cardunculus* has spiky heads of artichoke flowers that make a bright combination sandwiched between *Helenium* 'Sahin's Early Flowerer' and *Kniphofia* 'Prince Igor' in the Dell Garden in late summer. Although the flowers are identical, this form, *C. c.* var. *ferocissima*, has more strongly divided leaves than the species.

Further Recommendations

Some of the 1966 Bressingham introductions are much shorter than 'Lucifer', with C. 'Bressingham Blaze', a free-flowering reddish orange, and C. 'Spitfire', a more yellow-orange, both reaching only 60 cm (2 ft.) with a mass of densely held flowers in late summer. C. 'Vulcan', also 60 cm (2 ft.), has a more open spreading habit, the small scarlet-crimson flowers strikingly contrasted with a yellow throat. C. 'Firebird' bears a much closer resemblance to one if its parents, *C. masoniorum*, with large glowing orange-red flowers on graceful arching stems against bright green bladed leaves, making a striking display to 90 cm (3 ft.). C. 'Jenny Bloom', named after my youngest half-sister, has more of an upright branching habit to 90 cm (3 ft.), the freely produced small yellow flowers continuing for weeks in late summer. These summer-flowering selections can be considered hardy in **Z** 8–9, and to **Z** 7, at least with adequate winter protection, as mentioned under C. 'Lucifer'.

Cynara cardunculus

cardoon

Ornamental as a foliage and flowering plant, the silver-leaved cardoon is a versatile and reasonably hardy perennial.

This striking thistle-leaved hardy perennial belongs, somewhat strangely, to the *Aster* family and originates from north Africa across the whole of the northern Mediterranean regions, growing on open rocky slopes and dry grassland, sustained in summer by deep thong-like roots. It is an outstanding foliage plant with long, deeply dissected silvery grey leaves serving as a canopy for tall 150–180-cm (5–6-ft.) branching stems and large globe-shaped thistle heads topped with a mass of short violet-blue petals. Attractive to bees, the flowerheads remain a feature through autumn and winter as they finally fall apart.

↑
These maturing, fine inflorescences of *Deschampsia cespitosa* 'Goldtau' are in their late summer gold phase next to *Helenium* 'Bruno', with another group shown in the distance at Foggy Bottom.

The cardoon will grow on most soils, but needs good winter drainage. Where happy, it will be quite vigorous, and is best divided and planted in mid to late spring. Once established, it is best left alone. Cover roots in cold areas with bracken, straw or conifer foliage. Both foliage and flowers can be cut, and although parts of the plant are edible, it is the similar globe artichoke *C. scolymus*, with greener leaves, that is more widely used for cooking.
1½–2 m (5–6 ft.) × 90–120 cm (3–4 ft.)
F mid to late summer
Z 6–9

Deschampsia cespitosa 'Goldtau'

tufted hair grass

The aptly named 'Goldtau' ('Golden Dew') is a compact and floriferous ornamental grass with a long period of interest.

A widespread and variable clump-forming species native to cool temperate regions of the northern hemisphere from eastern Asia, Europe and North America, *D. cespitosa* is found growing in damp meadows and open forest, and on stream banks and lakesides. It prefers cooler climates to hotter, drier areas, and grows well in full sun in the former, needing shade in the latter.

Like many other grasses, *D. c.* 'Goldtau' was first appreciated and selected by plantsmen and horticulturists in Germany. New, narrow dark green leaves come into early growth and are soon followed in early summer by panicles of fine inflorescences that become more billowy and cloud-like as they age, changing from green to gold and then, in autumn, to beige. The harvest gold of summer is enhanced by dew on damp mornings, and turned to a sparkling silver magic by autumn frosts. Like that of *D. c.* and its other cultivars, the foliage of 'Goldtau' is semi-evergreen in milder climates, but any old or dead material should be cleaned out in early spring, trimming back remaining foliage by a third. Named cultivars can be divided in early spring or early autumn and, unless required, any seedlings that will be variable to the parent, removed.
45–60 cm (1½–2 ft.) × 60–75 cm (2–2½ ft.)
F early summer to late autumn
Z 4–9

←
Fresh green lacy foliage of *Dicentra* 'Luxuriant' makes a good contrast to deep red flowers in late spring at Foggy Bottom.

→
Drooping pink petals surround the golden-tipped cones of *Echinacea purpurea* 'Kim's Knee High' to make a show in the Summer Garden at Bressingham. Young greenish cones and erect petals are soon to change, continuing the long flowering season. Behind is *Stachys officinalis* 'Hummelo'.

Further Recommendations

Less compact than *D. c.* 'Goldtau' is *D. c.* 'Bronzeschleier' ('Bronze Veil') which grows to 90 cm (3 ft.) by as much across, with bronze-green inflorescences changing to bronze-gold, and the more upright *D. c.* 'Goldschleier' ('Gold Veil'), 120 cm (4 ft.), whose bright green airy heads turn to the gold of barley straw.

Dicentra 'Luxuriant'

fringed bleeding heart

Among a wealth of attractive *Dicentra* cultivars, 'Luxuriant' stands out as being reliable and long blooming, with bright green foliage and glowing red flowers.

The dicentras are classic spring- and summer-flowering perennials, for sun or shade where not too dry. Most selections, including *D.* 'Luxuriant', come from the two main North American species, *D. formosa* from the northwestern United States into British Columbia, and *D. eximea*, which is native to eastern North American from Nova Scotia to North Carolina, broadly following the Appalachian chain of mountains. *D. eximea* is clump forming, growing in damp soils in woodland usually in shade or semi-shade, and *D. formosa*, also a forest or woodland plant, has a spreading habit. Along with other subspecies, these form the parents of the many cultivars.

Dicentra 'Luxuriant' makes a spreading plant with suitably luxuriant fresh green finely divided leaves topped by a long display of heart-shaped glowing red flowers. With young plants and continued moist conditions flowering will carry into autumn, but in drought or dry situations flower and foliage will die back by late summer. Like other similar *Dicentra* cultivars it dislikes poor drainage, particularly in winter, and new plantings are generally best in spring. If clumps become congested with age their fleshy brittle roots are best divided and planted in early spring or early autumn, but divisions should not be too small. Keep moist until well established.

30–45 cm (1–1½ ft.) × 45–60 cm (1½–2 ft.)

F spring until late summer

Z 3–9

Further Recommendations

A few other cultivars deserve a mention. Good reds to consider are the vigorous *D.* 'Bacchanal', with blood-red flowers and contrasting bright green foliage, and *D.* 'Adrian Bloom', named for me by my father in 1976, which has crimson-red flowers and grey-green foliage. One of my favourite dicentras was named 'Pearl Drops' at Bressingham, but originated in Japan from nurseryman Dr. Rokujo. It is outstanding for its spreading silver-grey foliage, massed with pendulous white flowers, flushed with pink, in moist semi-shade lasting well into autumn. *D.* 'Langtrees', whose introduction followed a few years later, is similar if not identical, but either one is a good addition to the garden. All have similar dimensions and hardiness to *D.* 'Luxuriant', and are best in free-draining organic soils.

→

Robust, with sharply cut leaves, the small globe thistle *Echinops ritro* adds colour and variety to the perennial garden in summer, and is much appreciated by bees.

Echinacea purpurea 'Kim's Knee High'

purple coneflower

Easy to grow with a long and magnificent flower-to-frost performance, this is a sun-loving perennial to enjoy.

The echinaceas, all species of North American origin, are presently very fashionable and fast developing, with recent breeding activity producing some exciting new plants. It will take time to fully assess the gardenworthiness of all the new introductions, but *E. p.* 'Kim's Knee High' and others mentioned here, all arising directly from *E. purpurea*, the purple coneflower, have earned their laurels over many years.

E. purpurea is native to open woods and prairies from Virginia, northeast to Michigan and Iowa and south to Georgia and Louisiana, where it seeds freely and has a clumpy, slowly spreading rootstock. Hairy leaves, oval at the base and lance-shaped up the stem, are dark green and rough to the touch, the cone-headed flowers, rayed with purple, pink or white petals according to variety, a crowning glory in summer.

At around 60 cm (2 ft.), *E. p.* 'Kim's Knee High' is much shorter than

most early cultivars which typically reach 90–120 cm (3–4 ft.). Selected by Kim Hawkes of North Carolina, it has drooping clear pink petals accentuating an orange-bronze central cone, flowering from midsummer to early autumn. After these flowers fade and die to black in late autumn they remain attractive during winter, particularly when cones are covered with frost or snow. The seeds, appreciated in autumn by birds, will freely germinate in fertile surrounding soil in spring and can be hoed or kept as required as plants will not come true to the parent. To prevent seeding, stems should be cut back by mid to late autumn.

Like the species and all other cultivars of *Echinacea purpurea*, 'Kim's Knee High' prefers sun and is best planted in spring into reasonable soil with free drainage provided for summer and winter. All *E. p.* cultivars are heat and drought tolerant.
60 cm (2 ft.) × 45–60 cm (1½–2 ft.)
F midsummer to early autumn
Z 3–8

Further Recommendations
E. p. 'Kim's Knee High' needs no pruning, but some taller cultivars can

be trimmed back by half in early summer, reducing their eventual height and delaying summer flowering yet prolonging the autumn display. One such cultivar is the large rose-pink semi-double-flowered *E. p.* 'Magnus', raised in Sweden, which will reach 120 cm (4 ft.) or taller. Sturdier, to only 90 cm (3 ft.), is *E. p.* 'Robert Bloom', named after my brother, with only slightly drooping or reflexed petals of a deep purple-red. Of similar erect height and effect, the seed-raised *E. p.* 'Rubinstern' is outstanding for its large flattened ruby-red petals around a purple cone. White-flowered forms (how can they be "purple coneflowers", with green or yellow cones?) are striking, though less popular, adding coolness and contrast to the summer garden. *E. p.* 'White Lustre' and *E. p.* 'White Swan', both about 60–75 cm (2½–3 ft.) high, have cool white petals around yellow cones, while *E. p.* 'Kim's Mop Head', found as a sport on a plant of 'Kim's Knee High', exhibits the same characteristics as its parent, but with less reflexed white flowers around a greenish yellow cone.

I am excited about the rapid (and continuing) breeding work that has

been carried out on echinaceas in recent years. At Bressingham, we are trialling as many of the new cultivars as possible and it will be interesting to see which ones will have been proven truly gardenworthy in a decade's time.

Echinops ritro

small globe thistle

This undemanding thistle-like perennial adds contrast, curiosity and colour to the summer garden.

The Greek *echinops* means 'hedgehog-like', an apt description of the globe-shaped flowers on all of the species, some of which are too tall and floppy for garden use. *E. ritro* is native to Spain in the west across to Italy, Turkey and central Asia, growing on rocky open areas and scrub. In such dry conditions it reaches 30–60 cm (1–2 ft.), but expect 90–120 cm (3–4 ft.) in the garden. This sun-loving tap-rooted plant has dark green spiny leaves with white undersides, and in summer it produces rounded globes of deep blue flowers on sturdy spikes, much beloved by bees. A good cut flower, it also mixes very well in the garden with contrasting *Phlox paniculata* or *Helenium* or *Heliopsis*. The plants are adaptable to full sun or part shade with good drainage, and happy with poor soils since on moister, fertile types the stems may elongate and flop, and roots may spread more rapidly. Propagation is by seed or division, the latter best carried out in spring when plants can be tidied and pruned back. 90–120 cm (3–4 ft.) × 45–60 cm (1½–2 ft.)

F summer

Z 4–9

Further Recommendations

E. 'Veitch's Blue' is similar to *Echinops ritro* but re-blooms more freely. *E. r.* subsp. *ruthenicus* has mainly unbranched taller stems and steel-

→
The new leaves on evergreen, ground-covering *Epimedium ×perralchicum* 'Fröhnleiten' make a tapestry of bronze, purple and green in spring, with early morning sun filtering through the foliage.

blue flowers to 150 cm (5 ft.), and is reportedly less prone to spittlebugs where they are a problem.

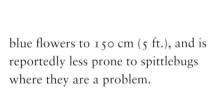

Epimedium ×perralchicum 'Fröhnleiten'

barrenwort

This tough, adaptable ground-covering evergreen perennial has exquisite spring flowers.

The common name of barrenwort does few favours to this genus of useful, attractive, mainly shade-loving perennials. Most species originate from northern Asia, with a few from Europe and one from North Africa, but as cultivars and species are somewhat promiscuous in their habits many of the garden cultivars have arisen as chance seedlings from mixed parents. A seedling selection from Germany, *E. ×p.* 'Fröhnleiten' arose from *E. ×perralchicum* (syn. *E. ×p.* 'Wisley') in an original chance cross at the Royal Horticultural Society's garden at Wisley between the evergreen North African species *E. perralderianum*, and *E. pinnatum* subsp. *colchicum* which is also evergreen, from northeast Turkey to nearby Georgia.

E. ×p. 'Fröhnleiten' forms dense mats of congested roots, able to withstand full sun in cooler summer climates and half shade in hotter regions. It is evergreen with glossy green, somewhat leathery mature leaves, to 30 cm (1 ft.), that are outshone by the emergence of new bronze-red spring foliage veined with bright green, darkening to summer green with coppery or bronze autumnal and winter tones. The clear yellow flowers, though seldom freely borne, are held on delicate spikes among and just above the foliage; they are worth a close look, with four petals rayed around smaller central petals and stamens. It may not be evergreen in all regions in every situation, as much will depend on cultural and local winter weather conditions. Free drainage and some shade, as long as plants are not drowned in autumn tree leaves, will give better protection than open or poorly drained situations.

Epimediums can be planted, and divided in early spring or early autumn. Firm in well on light or peaty soils, and water generously. Once established they are drought-resistant and grow well under trees. Deciduous forms and evergreens where foliage looks messy or tired should be cut back in late winter, in time for new flowers and leaves to appear.

30–45 cm (1–1½ ft.) × 30–45 cm (1–1½ ft.), spreading

F spring

Z 4–9

Further Recommendations

The broad large-leaved *E. pinnatum* and *E. p.* subsp. *colchicum* (the parent of *E. ×p.* 'Fröhnleiten') are both worthy, tough and attractive, mainly evergreen ground covers, both with yellow flowers, growing well in sun and shade. Both have similar details to *E. ×p.* 'Fröhnleiten'. *E. ×rubrum* is mainly evergreen, with striking bronze-red new leaves fading to light green with coppery brown tinges in autumn. The flowers, which show best when old foliage is removed, are rose-red with creamy white centres.

→
The American name of *Eryngium ×zabelii* 'Jos Eijking', *E. ×zabelii* 'Sapphire Blue', reflects its remarkably blue stems, topped by spiky bracts that surround the cones of flowers in summer—shown here against *Helenium* 'Pipsqueak' in the Summer Garden at Bressingham.

For flower and summer foliage the deciduous, woodland north Asian species *E. grandiflorum* is slower, but has first-class performers in *E. g.* 'Rose Queen', with bronze-tinged early foliage and deep rose-pink flowers; *E. g.* 'Lilafee', raised by German plantsman Ernst Pagels, with purple-bronze young growth and lilac-purple flowers; and the cool white, large-flowered *E. g.* 'White Queen', with light green foliage. All are 30–45 cm (1–1½ ft.) × 30–45 cm (1–1½ ft.), flowering spring, **Z** 5–9. This is another group of perennials undergoing change as new discoveries in the wild and recent hybridizing widens our choice.

Eryngium ×zabelii 'Jos Eijking'

sea holly, eryngo

Also known as *E. ×z.* 'Sapphire Blue' in North America, the blue stems and flowers in summer make this a stunningly exotic perennial.

Most of the 200+ species of sea holly have spiny leaf bracts, but few are native exclusively to seaside locations except the true sea holly, *E. maritimum*, a difficult plant to grow in the average garden. *E. ×zabelii* is a cross between the finely frilled *E. alpinum* and the blue-stemmed, silver-leaved *E. bourgatii*, the hybrid reaching 60–90 cm (2–3 ft.) with violet-blue cone-shaped heads circled by blue sharply pointed bracts. Most eryngiums make good cut flowers and those with deep blue stems are highly prized, so in 1993 I was delighted to work with Dutch cut flower breeder Wouter Ruigrok to introduce a striking new selection he had raised and named after a business colleague, Jos Eijking. Since its early introduction at the Chelsea Flower Show in 1995, it has proven itself to be a reliable and strikingly attractive plant.

From spiny green basal leaves emerge blue-green sturdy branched stems, the intensity of the blue developing from the top as silvery green heads and bracts also turn to violet-blue, opening to pale blue. The flowers are a great favourite of bees. Like most eryngiums *E. ×z.* 'Jos Eijking' is taprooted and sun-loving, and needs good drainage. Best planted in spring, most will last for years without disturbance.

They are excellent for cutting fresh or for drying, but also attractive into winter if left. In colder regions, foliage will disappear over winter; otherwise, clean before spring.

60–75 cm (2–2½ ft.) × 45–60 cm (1½–2 ft.)

F summer

Z 5–8

Further Recommendations

For the smaller or mediterranean-style dry garden, *E. bourgatii*, native to North Africa and Spain, offers low, narrow, spiny green and silver leaves and short 30–45-cm (1–1½–ft.) usually-blue stems, blue to green cones and silvery white bracts. *E. bourgatii* will be variable from seed, but *E. b.* 'Oxford Blue', *E. b.* 'Picos Blue' and *E. b.* 'Picos Amethyst' are good cultivar selections. All need sun and good drainage for longevity. 45–60 cm (1½–2 ft.) × 30–45 cm (1–1½ ft.), **F** summer, **Z** 5–8.

Eupatorium maculatum 'Gateway'

joe pye weed

This strong-growing perennial gives great garden presence late in the year—especially valuable in larger gardens.

The North American joe pye weeds are coming to be much appreciated for their stature, ease of cultivation and value to wildlife. *E. purpureum*, the green-stemmed joe pye weed, and *E. maculatum*, with purple-stained stems, are found primarily growing in damp places across eastern North America, the former with rounded purple flowerheads reaching as tall as 2½ m (8 ft.), the latter often nearly as tall with flatter heads of purple-pink flowers on strong leafy stems.

E. maculatum 'Gateway' is a North American selection from grass specialist Kurt Bluemel, with dark green lance-shaped leaves and, in full sun, erect purple stems that are branched with flattened heads as wide as 20 cm

(8 in.), with purple-pink flowers in late summer, much frequented by bees and butterflies. In moist conditions without earlier trimming it will reach 180 cm (6 ft.) or more in height, imposing and dominant in the late summer and autumn garden, with fluffy seedheads that stay attractive into winter. Used with ornamental grasses like *Miscanthus*, autumn *Aster* and *Helianthus*, *E. m.* 'Gateway' makes a fine specimen and backdrop to a reasonable-sized garden.

Now for the downsides: like similar *Eupatorium* cultivars, it makes a dense, almost impenetrable root system, spreading but not invasive— so this may need curbing in time. Secondly, they seed freely in most soils; these variable seedlings should be removed early. In drier conditions, lower foliage can deteriorate. If 1.6 m (5 ft.) or more is too high, pruning back growth by a third in early summer will reduce the eventual height, but expect flowers to be smaller. Stems

Few plants offer such an imposing late presence as this selection of joe pye weed, *Eupatorium maculatum* 'Gateway', shown here in late summer at Foggy Bottom. Accentuating its height is the lower-growing *Rudbeckia fulgida* var. *sullivantii* 'Goldsturm'.

→ The clump-forming cushion spurge, *Euphorbia polychroma*, adds brightness for many weeks in spring, associating well with blue-flowered pulmonarias.

are self-supporting even if they bend outwards after rainfall, and can be cut back when winter interest is at an end. Growth is usually late starting in spring.

180–240 cm (6–8 ft.)

F late summer to winter

Z 2–9

Further Recommendations

German selection *E. m.* 'Glutball' seems identical to 'Gateway', and *E. m.* 'Riesenschirm' is of similar stature to it but has deeper purple stems and flowers. For smaller gardens, I highly recommend a selection of the white snakeroot, *Eupatorium rugosum* 'Chocolate' (syn. *Ageratina altissima* 'Chocolate'), whose purple foliage has added great possibilities for those of us who like to play around with plant combinations. The species is native to woodland and open areas across eastern North America, with toothed oval leaves much smaller and lighter than the joe pye weeds. *E. p.* 'Chocolate' has green purple-tinged leaves deepening to mahogany-purple by summer, and without trimming a display of not-very-showy, off-white flowers appear in autumn on 150-cm (5-ft.) stems. Clump-forming for sun or shade where not too dry, preferring a spring planting, and likely to give best colour in sun (in my experience), these plants are best trimmed back in midsummer by 15 cm (6 in.) and again in late summer, dispensing with the flowers to make the most of the outstanding purple foliage. 120–150 cm (4–5 ft.) × 60–75 cm (2–2½ ft.), **F** late summer to autumn, **Z** 4–8.

Euphorbia polychroma

cushion spurge

A reliable and long-lived perennial spurge, *E. polychroma* is a glory in spring, green in summer and displays attractive seedheads in summer and autumn.

The spurges are a large and varied family, their origins across the world very much a guide to their garden use. All have a potentially harmful sticky white sap when propagated or damaged, so care should be taken to wear gloves when handling, as the sap can cause irritation to skin and eyes. Euphorbias are nonetheless fashionable, and some excellent deciduous and evergreen forms offer considerable choice.

E. polychroma (syn. *E. epithymoides*) is one of the hardiest and most reliable. The clump-forming species is native to southeastern Europe, where it grows in open woods and scrub. In early spring new leaves quickly form a mound of bright green foliage, topped by layers of green then yellow bract-like leaves and clusters of similarly coloured male and female flowers. The overall effect lasts for some weeks and this plant is one of the joys of spring, particularly when contrasted with blue spring-flowering pulmonarias or *Brunnera macrophylla* 'Jack Frost'. It will grow happily in most soils in sun or part shade where not too dry, lasting for years with very little attention, being drought tolerant but less happy in extreme heat and humidity. The late summer seeds are attractive, and in warmer summer regions where seeding is a problem, they can be lightly trimmed away with shears before they are ready to drop. Otherwise, a late winter or early spring cut back of old foliage is all that is necessary to prepare for the new season.
60 cm (2 ft.) × 60–75 cm (2–2½ ft.)
F spring to early summer
Z 4–8

Further Recommendations
For brighter yellow flowers, both *E. p.* 'Midas' and *E. p.* 'Sonnengold' are worthy choices. *E. p.* 'Candy' (syn. *E. p.* 'Purpurea'), with early foliage tinged purple, is a favourite of mine, yet likely to be surpassed by the newer, bronze-leaved *E. p.* 'Bonfire' which holds its striking colour all year. In habit and flowering time, they are similar to the species.

From the Kingdom of Bhutan and nearby in the Himalayas comes the striking but spreading *E. griffithii*, growing in open areas and near streamsides. It prefers moist, even heavy soils to lighter drier types where fleshy roots are more inclined to run. New spring growth, bracts and leaves are stained orange-red, particularly noticeable with the bronze-tinged leaves and luminous orange-red-flowered *E. g.* 'Dixter', named for Christopher Lloyd's Sussex garden. *E. g.* 'Fireglow' with a compact habit, green leaves and fiery orange flowers and raised at Bressingham is also first class. Both 90–120 cm (3–4 ft.) × 60–90 cm (2–3 ft.), spreading; flowering spring to early summer; **z** 5–8.

Festuca glauca 'Elijah Blue'

blue fescue

One of several first-class blue fescues that can play an important role in the garden, its startling blue foliage contrasting with many other plants.

There are innumerable named cultivars of *Festuca glauca*, a tuft-forming grass that originates in southern France. Most have similar characteristics: slender, needle-like leaves forming a clump of green to silver-blue foliage, the colour particularly intense in summer. Grown more for foliage than for flower, the early summer dainty inflorescences of blue or green, ripening to gold, are an attractive feature of selected cultivars. *Festuca glauca* 'Elijah Blue' was selected by Lois Woodhall at her Plantage Nursery on Long Island, no doubt partly for its

intense blue leaves, but also because it is a reliable grower.

The blue fescues are cool season grasses, prone to falling apart and dying in patches in hot humid climates. If they get old or, as often happens, infested with ants, they are best dug, split and replanted reasonably deeply, using only the best material. On the other hand, in cooler climates they may need division and replanting as seldom as every 5 years—best done in spring, when any old or dead foliage should be cleaned out. Once flowerheads are past their best in summer, these should also be pulled out. Preferring sun, the blue fescues are great fillers and also make dramatic contrasts to golden- or purple-leaved sun-loving shrubs such as *Spiraea*

japonica 'Magic Carpet' and *Cotinus coggygria* 'Royal Purple'.
30 cm (1 ft.) × 30 cm (1 ft.)
F spring to early summer
Z 4–8

Further Recommendations

I find it difficult to choose between 'Elijah Blue' and the German selection *F. g.* 'Blauglut' ('Blue Glow'), which has bright silver-blue foliage and a fine show of 'flowers'. Those two are similar in size, but for a slightly more compact selection try *F. g.* 'Blaufuchs' ('Blue Fox'), 15–20 cm (6–8 in.).

Gaura lindheimeri

wand flower

This long-flowering native American species, recently enhanced by many new selections, is still good garden value given sun and very good drainage.

Native to Louisiana and Texas, this prairie plant is reliably perennial on poor soils and with good winter drainage. It has a tufted rootstock and narrow dark green leaves, with slender 90–150-cm (3–5-ft.) stems holding pink buds, opening to white butterfly-like flowers that fade to pink as they age. The flowers, continuing from late spring until autumn, are directly attached to the stems which billow gracefully even in light breezes. In

←

In this sunny, dry position in the Dell Garden, the North American native wand flower, *Gaura lindheimeri*, blooms all summer--- here sandwiched between *Aster pyrenaeus* 'Lutetia' (foreground) and *A.* 'Little Carlow'.

→

With clusters of early summer flowers rising above aromatic foliage, *Geranium macrorrhizum* 'Bevan's Variety' shows its usefulness as a ground cover beneath a cedar in Foggy Bottom.

more fertile or even dry conditions, taller stems may flop later in the season, but *Gaura lindheimeri* can be trimmed back by 15 cm (6 in.) if required two or three times in the summer, and will continue to flower freely into autumn. In cooler, moister climates, planting in sun near tree roots will usually provide reasonably good winter drainage. The species and its cultivars are best planted in spring and are of course tolerant of heat and drought, seeding freely under the right conditions.

90–150 cm (3–5 ft.) × 60–90 cm (2–3 ft.)

F early summer until autumn

Z 5–9

Further Recommendations

Despite a reputation for being short-lived, gauras remain popular; except for the variegated-leaved forms, they fit in well with other sun-loving perennials and ornamental grasses. New introductions seem to occur every year, but *G. l.* 'Whirling Butterflies', a sterile non-seeding cultivar with large white flowers, usually growing to 90 cm (3 ft.) or less, is an outstanding selection.

The first pink-flowered cultivar came some years ago from Siskiyou Rare Plant Nursery in northern California. *G. l.* 'Siskiyou Pink' has red-stained stems and deep wine-red buds opening to pretty pink flowers centred by long white stamens. At 60 cm (2 ft.), it is shorter and sturdier than the species.

Geranium macrorrhizum 'Bevan's Variety'

bigroot geranium

With aromatic semi-evergreen foliage and bold flowers, this hardy geranium is excellent and adaptable for ground cover and can be relied on in any garden.

The popularity of hardy geraniums in recent years has been contagious. In 1960 there were perhaps 30 species and cultivars on offer, but today there are around a thousand and the choice is becoming too large and confusing—so I am limiting this list to a few tried-and-tested recommendations.

G. macrorrhizum is a vigorous, spreading but noninvasive perennial, native to southern European alpine regions where it grows in rocky open and wooded areas. It is very hardy and is adaptable to full sun and moist soils as well as very dry shade, making leafy carpets of 5-lobed dark to mid-green aromatic (some say pungent) leaves. Various selections have been collected in the wild or raised from seed with shades of white, pink, red to magenta as the colour range.

G. m. 'Bevan's Variety' was collected in the wild by Dr. Roger Bevan and has the deepest, almost shocking, magenta flowers held on slender stems above the foliage in pendulous or nodding clusters. Thick spreading roots below ground, and similarly robust stems above, both of which are easily curbed, are clothed in a summer carpet of green foliage. The main spring and early summer show of flowers continues more spasmodically until late summer. Depending on climate and positioning, the leaves

→

A small group of *Geranium* 'Rozanne' flows naturally beneath the brightly variegated foliage of *Miscanthus sinensis* 'Variegatus' in Foggy Bottom in midsummer. A few magenta flowers from a seedling of *Geranium psilostemon* appear in the foreground.

are often tinged with red in autumn; in warmer winter regions, the plants remain leafy through much of winter. They can thrive on almost any soil, in sun or shade. In spring, lift and divide if required.

25–40 cm (10–16 in.) × 45–60 cm (1½–2 ft.)

F early to midsummer

Z 4–9

Further Recommendations

Other recommended *G. m.* cultivars, similar in size to 'Bevan's Variety', include *G. m.* 'Album', with lighter green leaves, pink calyxes and white flowers, *G. m.* 'Ingwersen's Variety', with soft pink flowers, and *G. m.* 'Spessart', white with contrasting pink stamens.

With similar adaptability for most soils, sun or shade to the large-leaved and vigorous *G. macrorrhizum* and cultivars, the smaller-leaved hybrid *G.* ×*cantabrigiense* 'Cambridge' is ideal. It arose as a cross between *G. macrorrhizum* and *G. dalmaticum* in Cambridge University Botanic Garden, hence its name, and makes a low carpet of glossy green, subtly aromatic leaves and a free display of deep pink flowers. In this same category there

is *G.* ×*c.* 'Biokovo', pink with deeper pink stamens, and *G.* ×*c.* 'St. Ola', white fading to pink. All are excellent, trouble-free plants, good for edging, as ground cover or beneath deciduous shrubs. All 25–30 cm (10–12 in.) × 30–45 cm (1–1½ ft.), **F** summer, **Z** 4–9.

If you want tough, hardy, low-growing geraniums, the bloody cranesbill *Geranium sanguineum* and its cultivars take some beating. From slowly spreading roots they make mounds of deep green, finely divided foliage and are massed in early summer with shades of pink, purple, red and white finely veined flowers, hardy and drought- tolerant, for sun or light shade. Among the many cultivars available consider *G. s.* 'Alan Bloom' which I named for my father in 1992, a pleasing bright pink, 30 cm (1 ft.). *G. s.* 'John Elsley', named by my father for the well-known U.S.-based British plantsman, is a vigorous plant to 30–45 cm (1–1½ ft.), mauve-pink with purple veins, and *G. s.* var. *striatum* 'Splendens', low to 20 cm (8 in.) and spreading, with pale pink, crimson veined flowers, is tough yet delicate-looking.

Geranium 'Rozanne'

cranesbill

For impact, versatility and flowering performance, there are few hardy perennials to match the remarkable *Geranium* 'Rozanne'.

It arose in 1989 as a seedling in the garden of the late Donald and Rozanne Waterer in the village of Kilve, Somerset, England, the parents being the early-flowering *G. himalayense* and the later- and freely-flowering *G. wallichianum* 'Buxton's Variety', both species native to the Himalayas. The Waterers, being keen gardeners, knew this new hybrid was special and contacted me in 1991 to see if Blooms would trial and introduce it. The rest is history, but over the years *G.* 'Rozanne' has exceeded expectations, proving itself hardy, heat-tolerant and extremely long-blooming. In New Zealand's Auckland Botanic Garden it flowers all year long.

Geranium 'Rozanne' has a clumpy but rather scrawny root system and in spring new mid-green lobed and divided leaves soon make a mound of foliage before flowers open in early summer. Flowers are large, 5 cm (2 in.) across and, depending on age and

sunlight, blue to violet-blue, each of the 5 petals veined with purple into a white-suffused purple centre. Flowers continue to appear with abundance until autumn frosts, particularly in regions with cooler summers, for although tolerant of heat and drought, flowers will diminish in size and quantity in these conditions, fully recovering for a further burst in autumn.

G. 'Rozanne' will make a 90-cm (3-ft.) mound when established, so allowance must be made when planting. Later in summer new growth emerges from the centre and old or untidy foliage can then be tidied up if required; otherwise, cut back all foliage when it has died back in winter. G. 'Rozanne' grows well on a variety of soils in sun or part shade where not too dry. Its long flowering performance allows it to be displayed in patio containers, hanging baskets and even window-boxes. Try it as a 'river' or flowering ground cover, perhaps in association with roses.
60–90 cm (2–3 ft.) × 90–120 cm (3–4 ft.)
F from early summer to late autumn
Z 5–9

Further Recommendations
For large mound-forming cultivars consider G. 'Brookside', whose smaller-leaved foliage has a more airy appearance than G. 'Rozanne' and a succession of white-centred, dark violet-blue flowers, freely intermingling with nearby plants throughout summer. Sun or shade, 60–75 cm (2–2½ ft.) × 90–120 cm (3–4 ft.), **Z** 5–8.

G. 'Patricia', raised by Orkney breeder Alan Bremner, is also robust and somewhat brazen, with broad-lobed hairy leaves and bright magenta dish-shaped flowers, stained purple in the centre. It is a hot summer colour to use against blue and white flowers or grey or silver foliage, in sun or part shade. 75–90 cm (2½–3 ft.) × 90–120 cm (3–4 ft.), **F** summer with occasional re-bloom, **Z** 5–8.

Although slow to establish and needing shade in hotter climates, G. 'Blue Sunrise' has golden, red-tinged early growth and later, according to sun exposure, yellow-green to yellow leaves, the yellow holding up well in autumn even in shade, making a pleasing contrast to lavender fading to light blue flowers which continue from early summer to autumn. In hotter climates shade is recommended. Suitable for any

soil where not too dry. 60 cm (2 ft.) × 90–120 cm (3–4 ft.) once established, **F** summer to autumn, **Z** 6–8.

Finally, despite being brief in flower, the early woodland species, European native G. sylvaticum, the wood cranesbill, and its North American counterpart G. maculatum, the spotted cranesbill, are worth garden space. Both G. s. 'Mayflower', with deep lavender-blue, white-centred flowers, and G. s. 'Album' are first class. G. sylvaticum seeds particularly freely, and G. maculatum has a slowly spreading semi-woody rootstock, light green leaves and lilac-to-pink flowers. Both species will be happy in sun in colder climates; otherwise shade where not too dry is preferred. Both 60–75 cm (2–2½ ft.) × 45–60 cm (1½–2 ft.), **F** spring to early summer, **Z** 4–8.

Gillenia trifoliata

bowman's root, Indian physic

A long-lived gardenworthy perennial, G. trifoliata adds grace, charm and fragrance to any garden.

Native to eastern North America from New England west to Ontario, south to Georgia and west to Missouri

←
Dainty white flowers in summer are only part of the attraction of the easily grown, long-lived *Gillenia trifoliata*.

Hakonechloa macra 'Alboaurea'

golden variegated hakone grass

It would be difficult to overpraise this ornamental grass for the effect it brings to the year-round garden.

The only species in the genus, *H. macra* comes from Honshu, the main island of Japan, where it grows in moist, mountainous areas, on cliffs and hillsides, including Mount Hakone after which it was named. Growing from 45 cm (1½ ft.) to 90 cm (3 ft.) depending on its situation, the species deserves attention for its narrow, graceful, arching rich green leaves that make billowy mounds of foliage.

The golden variegated hakone grass, *H. m.* 'Alboaurea', which no doubt arose as a sport or mutation in Japan many years ago, may have a difficult name, but it is generally an easy, eye-catching and trouble-free plant to add drama to any garden. It forms a dense, slowly spreading clump of congested wiry roots, new deep yellow-and-green-striped shoots quickly emerging to make gently arching hummocks of bright golden ground-covering foliage.

There is no end to the uses and plant combinations possible with *H. m.* 'Alboaurea', as pathway edging, as

where it grows in open woodland and on rocky slopes and roadsides, *Gillenia trifoliata* is an adaptable plant with a woody rootstock. Once established, it will live for years with little maintenance. Its erect, reddish stems are clothed with dark green trifoliate leaves, above and among which in early summer a mass of butterfly-like fragrant white flowers dance on the breeze. When flowers fade the red brown seed capsule or calyx continues to add interest, generally followed by good autumn leaf colour. This is an unusual free-flowering plant for sun or light shade where not too dry—the warmer the climate, the more shade required. Cut back, lift and divide well-established plants only if necessary in spring (since *Gillenia trifoliata* is best grown from seed), and firm springy roots in well when planting. 90–120 cm (3–4 ft.) × 60–75 cm (2–2½ ft.)

F early to late summer

Z 5–9

ground cover beneath trees or shrubs where not too dry, combined with a blue hosta or black-leaved *Ophiopogon*, or grown in a container with foliage cascading down on all sides. Wispy flowers occur in late summer among the sometimes-red-tinted foliage, and even when this dies back, the thin brown-beige winter leaves remain attractive well into winter, continuously moved by wind and breeze. These are adaptable plants, but it is worth finding them a spot where not too hot and dry, in sun or shade according to climate. They can take heat but not extreme heat, sun and drought, requiring some moisture at the roots (when leaves curl, you know they need water). Open up heavier soils with leaf mould, composted bark or humus to allow roots to run freely. Divide plants in early spring before leaves have opened, not allowing them to dry out, and replant, firming in wiry roots, watering and lightly mulching. Cut back old foliage when it begins to break down in late winter.

30–45 cm (1–1½ ft.) × 45–60 cm (1½–2 ft.)

F late summer

Z 5–9

Further Recommendations

H. m. 'Alboaurea', which has white splashed on its gold-and-green leaves, is often confused with *H. m.* 'Aureola' which does not, but the two are mixed in the trade and equally worthy. *H. m.* 'Allgold', with purely golden-yellow leaves, is slightly prone to sun scorch so does best in some shade. Attractive though less dramatic is *H. m.* 'Albovariegata', with light green and creamy white striped leaves. All are of similar stature and hardiness to *H. m.* 'Alboaurea'.

Helenium 'Moerheim Beauty'

sneezewort, Helen's flower

One of the best of the *Helenium* hybrids, 'Moerheim Beauty' is a consistent performer, adding its rich colours to the summer garden.

Few of the original species of *Helenium* are grown by gardeners today; *H. autumnale*, widespread across North America, and *H. bigelovii* from California and Oregon provided the parentage for mostly European breeders to develop some colourful cultivars—clump-forming plants with narrow mid-green leaves, strong semi-woody branched stems (although some are inclined to flop), bearing

←

Hakonechloa macra 'Alboaurea' lights up a planting association at the zu Jeddeloh garden in Germany. In front of this most useful and decorative of grasses is *Heuchera* 'Silver Scrolls', with *Geranium* 'Rozanne' growing beneath the purple leaves of *Actaea simplex* 'Brunette' behind. Shown in early summer, this combination will remain attractive until winter.

→

The warmth of high summer is reflected in the rich-toned flowers of the early- and long-flowering sneezewort, *Helenium* 'Moerheim Beauty'.

distinctive heads of variously coloured flowers, each with a central short button-like cone.

H. 'Moerheim Beauty' was raised by the famous Dutch Moerheim nurseries and introduced in 1930, standing the test of time. One of the earliest to flower, its erect 75–90-cm (2½–3-ft.) stems produce a succession of orange-brown daisy-like flowers, the petals expanding to circle the central rounded disc that deepens from reddish green to deep brown. It provides great contrast to perennials such as *Phlox paniculata*, *Agapanthus* and *Monarda* and fits in well with ornamental grasses. Easy to grow on most soils in sun, it is better with some moisture than when too dry. Some heleniums are inclined to get tall and leggy, so pruning a third of new growth in early summer with shears will reduce height and increase the number of flowers although it may delay flowering. Cut away mildew-infected stems later in summer as necessary; by midwinter, cut stems back to the ground. If plants are congested after a few years, divide in early spring, keeping younger material to replant.

75–90 cm (2½–3 ft.) × 45–60 cm (1½–2 ft.)
F early to late summer
Z 3–9

Further Recommendations

In addition to *Helenium* 'Moerheim Beauty', I recommend *H*. 'Butterpat', with light green leaves and deep yellow rayed petals around a green, turning-to-gold centre, and *H*. 'Coppelia', which has a sturdy erect habit and neat coppery orange flowers with a brown centre, both 75–90 cm (2½–3 ft.) tall and raised at Bressingham around 1960.

Karl Foerster, a well-known gardener and nurseryman from Germany, also raised many good hybrids including the compact *H*. 'Blütentisch',

golden-yellow flowers streaked reddish brown with a brown centre, 75–90 cm (2½-3 ft.), and the taller *H.* 'Königstiger' which has striking golden-yellow petals margined reddish brown with a brown centre, 120–150 cm (4–5 ft.). Lastly consider two more dwarf selections, the early-flowering *H.* 'Wyndley', brown-centred with golden-yellow-suffused reddish brown petals, 45–75 cm (1½–2½ ft.) and the free-flowering *H.* 'Pipsqueak', only 45–60 cm (1½ –2 ft.) tall, with pendulous petals falling away from a central brown cone. All described flower early to late summer. **Z** 3–9.

Helianthus 'Lemon Queen'

sunflower

This reliable and robust perennial is guaranteed to give a long display of autumn flowers.

Like *Eupatorium maculatum* 'Gateway', joe pye weed, to which it is a perfect partner, *Helianthus* 'Lemon Queen' is not for the small garden; reaching 180–240 cm (6–8 ft.), it is reliable and showy. It makes a slowly spreading, non-invasive clump with rather coarse green leaves on extending stems, finally displaying pleasing 5-cm (2-in.) wide lemon-yellow petals around an orange-yellow centre in late summer or early autumn. Like the eupatorium, this is a specimen plant and needs space around it. Best in full sun in most soils where not too dry, although it will withstand drought once established. For a shorter, bushier plant, trim back new stems by half in midsummer, but in the larger or natural garden, its height is an advantage as it displays yellow flowers against a blue autumn sky. Divide or reduce clumps in spring if necessary every few years. 180–240 cm (6–8 ft.) × 120–150 cm (4–5 ft.)
F late summer to autumn
Z 3–9

Heliopsis helianthoides var. scabra 'Spitzentänzerin'

oxe eye, false sunflower

Sun-loving, long-flowering and easy to grow, this cultivar will brighten up the garden in summer.

The long name should not deter us from appreciating the gardenworthy heliopsis, another North American native that was taken to Europe to be appreciated and hybridized. *H. helianthoides*, the ox eye, originates from eastern North America across to Ontario and south to Georgia, growing in open scrub and woodland edges in sunny places. It has erect stems, dark green irregularly cut leaves and orange to yellow sunflower-like flowers all summer. Clump-forming, it grows on most soils where neither too wet nor too dry, and once established it is reasonably drought tolerant.

H. h. var. *s.* 'Spitzentänzerin' (in English, 'Ballerina') was bred by German plantsman Karl Foerster and

A large group of the robust perennial *Helianthus* 'Lemon Queen' makes an autumn show in Adrian's Wood, a garden devoted to North American plants at Bressingham. *Aster novae-angliae* is in the foreground, while *Eupatorium maculatum* is in the the midst of *H.* 'Lemon Queen'.

→

The semi-double flowers of *Heliopsis helianthoides* var. *scabra* 'Spitzentänzerin' make a bright splash of colour for weeks in summer alongside *Campanula lactiflora* and *Helenium* 'Moerheim Beauty'.

introduced in 1949. It has overlapping semi-double golden yellow petals and a yellow-green centre turning to gold on 120-cm (4-ft.) stems. In cooler, moister climates some heliopsis can get leggy, although unless crowded by other plants or in half shade they normally remain erect. These plants are generally good for cutting. Early summer trimming of growth by half will reduce height but it will also delay flowering. Young plants or seedlings are not always robust until established, so they are best planted in spring in well-drained soil. Divide large clumps as necessary every few years, also in spring.
120–150 cm (4–5 ft.) × 60–90 cm (2–3 ft.)
F mid to late summer
Z 4–9

Further Recommendations
H. h. var. *s.* 'Sommersonne' ('Summer Sun'), 120–150 cm (4–5 ft.) tall, is a popular single with orange-yellow petals. In doubles, two worth looking for are *H. h.* var. *s.* 'Goldgefieder ('Golden Plume'), 120 cm (4 ft.) tall, and one of my favourites: *H. h.* var. *s.* 'Goldgrünherz' ('Goldgreenheart'),

shorter at 90 cm (3 ft.), with bright yellow flowers, double with a greenish centre. Whether you like it or not, you cannot deny that *H. h.* LORAINE SUNSHINE 'Helhan', raised by Brent Hanson in Wisconsin, has great impact, with its creamy white leaves veined with green, contrasting (many might say clashing) with golden-yellow flowers on 90–120-cm (3–4-ft.) stems: eye-catching, but takes time to get established.

Helleborus ×hybridus

Lenten rose

Whether in sun or shade, these hybrids give magnificent late winter to spring flowers, with attractive foliage to follow.

The majority of these beautiful late-winter-flowering perennials are grown from seed and produce some variance. I would be hard-pressed to recommend a single named cultivar since these they are mostly produced by the slow process of division. So deservedly

popular have they become in all temperate gardening countries that personal choice can easily be made, knowing that generally success will be achieved.

Before 1998 most hybrids were listed under *H. orientalis*, the Lenten rose, but this was considered botanically incorrect since as many as nine species have been involved in giving rise to these hybrids. There is now a multitude of flower choice: black, purple-red, grey-blue, pink, green, white, even speckled; double, semi-double and single flowers, narrow and broad petals, outward- and downward-facing flowers, mostly with attractive central yellow or golden stamens—a veritable feast for the gardener.

All form gradually expanding clumps with mostly dark green leathery leaves to 30–45 cm (1–1½ ft.), making good ground cover from spring to winter when planted in groups. Depending on personal choice and their condition, old leaves are best cut away in late autumn or early winter before new flowers and leaves

emerge in late winter. Divide with care on established clumps in autumn, remembering that plants of *Helleborus* are poisonous if ingested and an irritant to the skin, so wearing gloves may be advisable.

H. ×hybridus will grow in any reasonable organic soil where not too dry, in sun or shade, and once established will withstand drought. In hotter summer regions they are more likely to require shade than in cooler climates, but in all cases good winter drainage is preferred. When flowers have finished on selected cultivars, you may wish to cut away seedheads before self-seeding can occur as they will not come true to the parent, but otherwise young seedlings that arise (and there may be many) can be grown for a season and then planted elsewhere in the garden. In late winter or early spring good garden centres or nurseries often have a choice of plants in flower that you can personally select from the various seed strains available, which surely offer good value. These are indispensable

←
Deep-maroon-flowered *Helleborus* ×*hybridus* blooms for weeks in early spring, its stems and pendulous flowers rising above the pulmonarias at Foggy Bottom.

plants for the year-round garden; once planted, they stay for years with little maintenance.

30–60 cm (1–2 ft.) × 45–60 cm (1½–2 ft.)

F late winter to spring

Z 4–9

Hemerocallis 'Hyperion'

daylily

Among the daylilies, which vary so greatly in colour and appearance, I must recommend the classic and reliable *H.* 'Hyperion'.

So ubiquitous are daylilies in North America—literally thousands of cultivars are available, with hundreds of new varieties introduced each year—that you'd be forgiven for assuming them to be North American natives. Yet the 20 or so species of *Hemerocallis* actually originate from China, Japan and Korea, growing in moist areas in open fields or woodland edges. The species, most of which have fragrant trumpet-shaped flowers in shades of orange and yellow, exhibit a natural charm above bright green, grassy foliage, and the old and continuously popular hybrid *H.* 'Hyperion' shares these qualities. Introduced as long ago as 1924, 'Hyperion' has lemon-yellow, highly fragrant flowers held on 90-cm (3-ft.) green stems for a few weeks in midsummer. It is ideal in sun or light shade where not too dry.

90 cm (3 ft.) × 60–75 cm (2–2½ ft.)

F summer

Z 3–9

Further Recommendations

Daylilies are clump-forming plants, and can be as short as 30 cm (1 ft.) and as tall as 2 m (6 ft.) in flower, with a wide range of flower sizes, shapes and colours, some exquisitely marked and shaded and others brash and vulgar, depending on your opinion. In the garden they can be quite difficult to use, as flowers (without daily deadheading) and later foliage (without constant cleaning) can look shabby. The more natural-looking, smaller-flowered forms can be used in drifts, but larger-flowered selections of choice can work well as small specimen groups of the same kind, with shrubs or ornamental grasses. Older clumps get congested and need division every few years.

Dwarf repeat-flowering cultivars, including the golden-yellow *H.* 'Stella de Oro', need dividing every two or three years. Kept young on fertile soil that does not dry out, the small, fragrant flowers of this most popular of all daylilies, 45–60 cm (1½–2 ft.) tall, will continue all summer and into autumn. Also dwarf, repeat-blooming and fragrant are lemon-yellow *H.* 'Happy Returns', and *H.* 'Pardon Me' with bright red, yellow-centred

←
Hemerocallis 'Hyperion' introduced in 1924, has long been a popular classic for its cheerful, fragrant and natural flowers.

→
More purple than chocolate-coloured in spring growth, a mass of tiny flowers and a long season of attractive foliage are still to come on *Heuchera* 'Chocolate Ruffles'.

reliable, group of garden plants have been highly bred in recent years, all from North American native species including *H. cylindrica* and *H. micrantha* from the northwest and *H. americana* and *H. villosa* from the eastern regions, growing mostly in hilly or mountainous areas, withstanding heat and cold, but all generally where good drainage exists. Depending on climate, most make evergreen or semi-evergreen clumps, the species and cultivars ranging from miniature alpine or rock plants to large-leaved, 90-cm (3-ft.) flowering perennials, their flowers often insignificant in size and colour.

H. 'Chocolate Ruffles', bred by *Heuchera* specialist Dan Heims, is a reliable, long-lived heuchera with great foliage appeal for most of the year (climate permitting). It forms 30–45-cm (1–1½-ft.) mounds of ruffled leaves, reddish chocolate on the upper side and deep purple-red beneath, with a good summer display of small purplish flowers on 60–75-cm (2–2½-ft.) purple stems.

A good doer in a range of soils and climates, 'Chocolate Ruffles' holds colour well in heat, but afternoon shade in hotter climates will help

blooms, both reaching 45 cm (1½ ft.). Also dependable, raised by the same German breeder and considered to be classics are the midsummer-flowering *H.* 'Corky', which has relatively small bell-shaped pale yellow flowers opening from reddish brown buds, retaining a bronze reverse to the petals, and the similar slightly shorter *H.* 'Golden Chimes', with mahogany-brown stems and buds, and golden-yellow petals. Both are natural-looking, free-flower-

ing perennials, 60–75 cm (2–2½ ft.) tall. All **Z** 3–9.

Heuchera 'Chocolate Ruffles'

alum root, coral bell

A striking and consistent performer, *H.* 'Chocolate Ruffles' holds its own against a plethora of new introductions.

This popular, though not always

→

In its early stages and in semi-shade, *Hosta* 'Halcyon' has early summer leaves of ethereal blue, with scalloped foliage accentuating its architectural quality.

to prevent leaf scorch that comes with heat and drought. Good winter drainage will help longevity in cooler, wetter regions. Like other heucheras, the plants have a tendency to become woody with age and crowns can lift out of the soil, so division in spring, discarding old wood and replanting younger pieces into moist, friable soil, firming well, and lightly mulching will rejuvenate. On some foliage cultivars, insignificant flowers can be removed on sight if preferred, while on others deadheading spent flower stalks will prolong flowering. Heucheras with good flowers are excellent for flower-arranging.

75 cm (2½ ft.) × 45–60 cm (1½–2 ft.)
F summer
Z 4–9

Further Recommendations

The earliest purple-leaved cultivar, *H. micrantha* var. *diversifolia* 'Palace Purple', was raised and named around 1980 by Kew Gardens in England, and sold as a variable seed strain. The unreliability of this led me to select from hundreds of seedlings at Bressingham a large crinkled purple-bronze-leaved plant that I called *H. m.* var. *d.* 'Bressingham Bronze',

so gardeners could be sure of what they were getting. Although effective, it is less dependable and versatile than *H.* 'Prince' which makes a low mound of deep-bronze-purple leaves, and creamy white flowers 60–75 cm (2–2½ ft.) tall; *H.* 'Plum Pudding', with insignificant flowers but glossy purple-red foliage withstanding heat; and the impressive *H.* 'Obsidian', with deepest black-purple leaves and a vigorous habit. For marbled foliage, I recommend the compact *H.* 'Can Can', whose early ruffled silvery leaves are veined with bronze, turning green in summer, with purple-red undersides, and insignificant flowers, and *H.* 'Silver Scrolls', with larger, more rounded bright silver leaves with distinctive bronze-purple veining, purple beneath, and white flowers. An outstanding selection from U.S. breeders Charles and Martha Oliver, *H.* 'Raspberry Ice' has silver veins, purple leaves and a long display of bright pink flowers on 45-cm (1½-ft.) stems.

Although the earlier selections of *H. cylindrica*, *H. brizoides* and *H. sanguinea* are less and less seen, they are still highly gardenworthy. My grandfather Charles Bloom and my father Alan selected and bred many varieties for

cut flower and garden: *H. sanguinea* 'Red Spangles', making a compact mound of green leaves and 45–60-cm (1½–2-ft.) spikes clustered with blood-red bell-shaped flowers, is one of the best, *H. brizoides* 'Pretty Polly' with soft pink pendulous flowers to 30 cm (1 ft.) one of the shortest, and *H. sanguinea* 'Rosemary Bloom', named after my wife with glowing pink, yellow-centred flowers continuing for weeks on 60-cm (2-ft.) spikes, is of course one of my favourites. All are summer flowering, **Z** 4–9. Finally, for effective and reliable ground cover in sun or shade (according to climate), consider *H. americana* 'Dale's Strain', a variable seed-raised selection by Pennsylvania nurseryman Dale Hendricks, 30 cm (1 ft.) high, with mounds of rounded green to bronze leaves marked with silver, flowers insignificant, **Z** 3–9.

Hosta 'Halcyon'

plantain lily

For foliage and flower in gardens of all sizes, or in a patio container, *Hosta* 'Halcyon' is peerless.

Despite some pest problems, hostas are popular and largely successful

→
On a semi-shaded bank in the Dell Garden at Bressingham in early summer, bold groups of hostas cover the slope, making a patchwork of various colours and sizes of leaves. In the front, left to right, are *H.* 'Francee', *H.* 'Sunpower' and *H. ventricosa* 'Gold Flush'. Central behind them is *H.* 'Piedmont', and *H.* 'Sum and Substance' is behind the cercis centre left.

because they are tough, hardy and adaptable to a range of soils and climates. New introductions each year add confusingly to the 5,000+ cultivars that have been named and introduced. These have all derived from the 40 or so species native to Japan, China and Korea, and except in cooler climates they are considered to be shade-loving plants with stout, fleshy rootstocks. They are grown mainly for their attractive lance- or heart-shaped leaves, with good flowers and fragrance seen as a bonus. New cultivars arise as mutations or sports on established plants or from micropropagation, while others are raised from seed although those bred from specific parents by *Hosta* breeders are more likely to be worthy of introduction. Most *Hosta* breeding has been done in the United States, but *Hosta* 'Halcyon' was raised in England, along with other good cultivars, by plantsman Eric Smith, a cross between *H. sieboldiana* 'Elegans' and *H. tardiflora*, its intense blue inherited from the former and lance-shaped leaves from the latter.

    H. 'Halcyon' makes a mound of overlapping medium-sized leaves, slightly scalloped and ribbed, followed in summer with a good display

of greyish white bell-shaped flowers clustered on 45-cm (1½-ft.) stems. From spring until autumn the plant remains attractive, the dying leaves briefly turning gold before autumn frosts. *H.* 'Halcyon' is a classic hosta for garden or container and lends itself to innumerable plant associations, in particular with *Hakonechloa macra* 'Alboaurea'.

Hostas are easy when given a reasonably moist fertile soil that doesn't dry out, although once well established they are fairly drought-resistant for a limited period. Regular mulching or the addition of organic compost to lighter soils will benefit. Slugs and snails are the scourge of hostas and if these are a continual problem one must either take every precaution (I find the most effective prevention is slug pellets) or, in the worst scenario, discontinue growing them. If early damage occurs through spring frost or slugs, the foliage can be cut to the ground; more will regrow if given adequate moisture, but leaves will be smaller. Once planted, hostas seldom need disturbing although old plants can become congested and will need dividing after many years, involving prising apart with two sturdy forks,

preferably in early spring before new shoots emerge.

foliage 30–45 cm (1–1½ ft.) × 90 cm (3 ft.), flowers 50 cm (just over 1½ ft.)
F midsummer
Z 3–9

Further Recommendations

All hostas recommended here are summer-flowering, and suitable for **Z** 3–9.

H. sieboldiana 'Elegans' was the first large blue-green selection introduced by Georg Arends in 1905, making a dense mound of overlapping puckered heart-shaped leaves; of similar size and habit are *H.* 'Big Daddy' and *H.* 'Bressingham Blue'. The architectural *H.* 'Krossa Regal', with elegant grey-blue upright, arching leaves and lavender flowers, is excellent for the container. All are slug-resistant and approximately 75 cm (2½ ft.) × 90 cm (3 ft.).

As specimens, large-leaved hostas make quite a statement and none more so than the pale-lavender-flowered, slug-resistant *H.* 'Sum and Substance', raised like so many other good cultivars by Paul Aden. Ribbed chartreuse glossy leaves, maturing to gold depending on sunlight, are as large as

45 cm (1½ ft.) × 38 cm (15 in.). Particularly effective in a container is *H.* 'Sagae' (syn. *H. fluctuans* 'Variegata'), a favourite of mine with an erect habit and well-spaced undulating mid green leaves, edged with gold that pales to cream in summer, and lavender flowers on 150-cm (5-ft.) spikes. Foliage on mature plants measures 75 cm (2½ ft.) × 120–150 cm (4–5 ft.).

H. 'Francee' starts into growth from striking purple, pointed buds, soon to open to deep green leaves, narrowly margined with white, and a good summer show of pale lavender flowers—an all-round dependable plant, from which the perhaps more striking *H.* 'Patriot' arose as a sport, displaying a wider contrasting white margin and flowers similar to those of 'Francee'. Both approximately 50 cm (20 in.) × 90 cm (3 ft.).

I have long rated *H.* 'Shade Fanfare', an easily grown, showy hosta with light green puckered leaves edged irregularly with cream to yellow which lights up a shady spot. Flowers are soft lavender. 50 cm (20 in.) × 90 cm (3 ft.). Lastly, the smaller-leaved classic *H.* 'Golden Tiara', almost a smaller, more mounded version of *H.* 'Shade Fanfare', has green heart-shaped over-

lapping leaves edged irregularly with chartreuse turning to gold, then fading to cream, with a good show of lavender-purple flowers above the foliage. 45 cm (1½ ft.) × 75–90 cm (2½–3 ft.)

Imperata cylindrica 'Rubra'

Japanese blood grass

Grown in the garden or a container, this ornamental grass creates stunning colour and drama for months.

The origin of this cultivar goes back many years to Japan, and although it will gradually spread on moist, fertile soils, it is quite unlike the invasive, banned, green-leaved weed *Imperata cylindrica*. In fact, on lighter, drier soils it can be quite difficult to establish, leading many to consider it less than hardy.

To me, it is a foliage plant to be treasured from the moment the green, narrow red-tipped leaves appear in spring from shallow spreading roots, reaching 30–45 cm (1–1½ ft.) by midsummer; from then until late autumn, the leaves in full light turn blood red, then crimson and finally a still attractive brown-beige after dying back after autumn frosts. Kurt Bluemel, well-known advocate of ornamental grasses, had called *I. c.* 'Rubra' by the catchy name of *I. c.* 'Red Baron', although considering its origins *I.c.* 'Red Shogun' might have been more appropriate.

It is best planted in spring to get established, and prefers moist soils. Lift, divide and replant, firming in well when new growth is under 5–10 cm (2–4 in.), not allowing the roots to dry out. Any wayward growth seen as undesirable can be curbed at this time too. It makes a great container plant, but is most effective as a flowing 'river', which is how I first saw it used in Kurt Bluemel's Maryland garden. 30–45 cm (1–1½ ft.) × 30 cm (1 ft.)
F seldom
Z 6–9

Siberian iris

The Siberian irises are one of the most useful and adaptable group of perennials, with *I. s.* 'Silver Edge' and other cultivars providing exquisite flowers to light up early summer.

In the wild the Siberian iris does not quite make it to Siberia, growing in damp meadows, streamsides and swampy areas from southwestern Europe across to the Balkans and southern Russia. In recent years plant breeders have transformed the range available to gardeners without discarding the charm of the smaller-flowered species. Most have green, grass-like or slightly broader, bladed leaves, with erect slender stems hold-ing flowers above as well as sometimes inside the foliage and, with recent breeding, occurring at heights from 45 cm (1½ ft.) to 120 cm (4 ft.).

While they prefer moist soils in full sun, plants will grow well in average garden soil that is not too free-draining or dry. That said, a waterside location is perfect culturally and aesthetically. Shade is tolerated, but flowering performance may suffer. Siberian irises soon form sturdy clumps but seldom need attention beyond cutting back old foliage in winter or early spring, although if clumps become old and congested, plants are best dug up, split and replanted with compost-improved soil, in early autumn or early spring.

I. s. 'Silver Edge' is a widely grown and popular hybrid with rich blue wavy-edged flowers, a white line finely etched around each petal, the centre veined white and yellow. Depending on climate, expect flowers from early summer for a few weeks only, but with later perennials to take over the colour, the green, grassy foliage and ripening seedheads still serve a useful purpose, with foliage often giving a brief brown or golden autumn tint. 60–75 cm (2–2½ ft.) × 60 cm (2 ft.)

F early to midsummer

Z 3–8

Further Recommendations

The choice of available cultivars varies from country to country, but tried-and-tested and fairly widely available are *I. s.* 'Shirley Pope', deep purple-

←

In early summer at Foggy Bottom, *Iris sibirica* 'Silver Edge' is a perfect foil for the deep pink bottlebrush heads of *Persicaria bistorta* 'Hohe Tatra'

red, 90 cm (3 ft.), *I. s.* 'Baby Sister', light blue, almost the shortest at 45 cm (1½ ft.), *I. s.* 'Flight of Butterflies', rather aptly named for masses of small violet-blue, white, purple-veined falls (lower petals), 90 cm (3 ft.), *I. s.* 'White Swirl', the first introduction in 1957 to have more open flared falls, wavy-edged snowy white and yellow, 1 m (3 ft.), and finally *I. s.* 'Butter and Sugar', a later introduction, shorter at 75 cm (2½ ft.) with creamy yellow and white flowers. There are many more in purple, blue and white—even edging on pink.

Kniphofia 'Percy's Pride'

Like all good plants, this outstanding late-flowering kniphofia is becoming more appreciated with time.

The kniphofias are a striking group of perennials belonging to the lily family, the majority of species originating in South Africa where they grow mostly in grassland at higher altitudes in mountainous regions. Their promiscuity in naturally interbreeding, helped by breeders, has led to a multitude of cultivar introductions, some with broad, lax leaves, others with grassy foliage and erect spikes from 45 cm (1½ ft.) to 180 cm (6 ft.) or taller, topped by poker-like heads of pendulous tubular flowers. Flowering times vary from late spring until late autumn, with shades of orange, red and yellow predominant, the developing flowers changing colour as they enlarge, opening from the base upwards followed swiftly by bees attracted to their nectar.

Generally kniphofias require well-drained soil in winter and reasonable moisture in summer, which in damper climates is not always easy to achieve. Wet winter conditions and fluctuations in temperature are likely to lead to more losses than in drier, colder weather. Mid spring planting is always recommended to enable fleshy root systems to become established, and this is the time to tidy up old foliage and divide plants if old or too congested, discarding any woody or rotting material; otherwise, if plants look happy, they can go undisturbed for several years. In colder climates, protect from frost penetration around the base by using straw or leaves to 10 cm (4 in.) depth and covering the remainder lightly with evergreen foliage, allowing the plant to breathe.

There are some excellent cultivars and it is nice to pay tribute to Percy Piper, after whom this classic *Kniphofia* is named, as he and Alan Bloom were instrumental in breeding some first-class selections at Bressingham. *Kniphofia* 'Percy's Pride' has good, rich green-bladed foliage and a long succession of densely packed green-tinted flowers opening from pale green buds, an architectural statement from late summer into autumn. Kniphofias are good for cutting, and deadheading spent flowers, cutting away at the base, should help to prolong flowering. 120 cm (4 ft.) × 60–90 cm (2–3 ft.) **F** late summer to autumn **Z** 6–8

Further Recommendations

The seasonal variation in kniphofias starts with the somewhat startling *K.* 'Atlanta' named after the Atlanta Hotel garden in Cornwall, England where it was discovered. It is striking but difficult to place, with red and yellow pokers on 120-cm (4-ft.) stems in mid to late spring. Next comes *K.* 'Shining Sceptre', 90–120 cm (3–4 ft.), almost orange-gold above deep green grassy foliage; the bright cheery yellow of *K.* 'Sunningdale Yellow',

←

In front of Bressingham Hall, a clump of the outstanding red hot (yellow) poker, *Kniphofia* 'Percy's Pride', makes a late summer show. It was raised by Alan Bloom and gardener Percy Piper, who did much of the hybridizing of new cultivars at Bressingham.

→

The low-growing shasta daisy, *Leucanthemum ×superbum* 'Snowcap', makes a sheet of dazzling white flowers to brighten up the garden in midsummer.

75 cm (2½ ft.); the Beth Chatto selection *K.* 'Green Jade', 120 cm (4 ft.), pale green opening to white; the tough *K. caulescens*, 90–120 cm (3–4ft.), smoky, glaucous-leaved, with burnished red tips, yellow beneath; *K.* 'Little Maid', 60 cm (2 ft.), also from Beth Chatto, with a succession of small poker heads, green in bud opening to creamy yellow in late summer and autumn; and *K.* 'Bressingham Comet', with grassy *K. galpinii*-inherited foliage and a long fiery display of orange, red-tipped flowers on 60-cm (2-ft.) spikes. Also late is *K.* 'Cobra', 90 cm (3 ft.), one I named at Bressingham for its rather sinister tightly clasped bronze buds, fading to copper, then yellow; and *K.* 'Brimstone', 90 cm (3 ft.), introduced around 1970 by respected nurseryman and plantsman Fred Barcock, with bright green, grassy leaves and a long and brilliant show of light yellow flowers. Lastly, few perennials can outdo the spectacular show of *K. rooperi* (syn. 'C.M. Prichard'), whose large globular heads of glowing orange-red open to yellow, standing on sturdy 120–150-cm (4–5-ft.) spikes. The majority are hardy **Z** 6–8, given cultural suggestions for *K.* 'Percy's Pride'.

Leucanthemum ×superbum 'Snowcap'

shasta daisy

This reliable, vegetatively produced shasta daisy gives a brilliant display of white yellow-centred flowers in summer.

Sometimes listed under *Chrysanthemum maximum* or *Chrysanthemum ×superbum*, shasta daisies are staple summer perennials, evocative of the traditional cottage garden or perennial border. Although botanists cannot fully agree on the complete parentage of the hybrids, the European native ox eye daisy, *Leucanthemum vulgare*, is believed to be one of them. We now have a wide choice of cultivars, single, semi-double and fully double, with broad to frilly, narrow, mostly white petals and yellow centres.

L. ×s. 'Snowcap' was a chance seedling at Bressingham, with dark green, glossy leaves and a bold display of horizontally held single white petals with a yellow centre on 30–40-cm (1–1⅓-ft.) stems creating an almost carpet-like effect. The sun-loving shasta daisies can be short-lived, usually growing vigorously and flowering freely, but roots become congested and

can die out in patches, particularly with poor winter drainage. Plants may need lifting, dividing and replanting in spring every 2 or 3 years. Younger plants will continue to flower all summer and into autumn with some deadheading. Some are inclined to sulk in hot, humid conditions, and without earlier trimming taller cultivars tend to flop unless staked. Early summer shearing of a third of new growth will help to reduce height and produce bushier plants. Most are excellent for cutting. Overall, then, these are showy plants that need some maintenance. 30–40 cm (1–1⅓ ft.) × 30–45 cm (1–1½ ft.)

F summer

Z 4–8

Further Recommendations

L. ×s. 'Snowcap' will not flop, of course, and nor will other dwarf selections such as the slightly variable, seed-raised *L. ×s.* 'Snow Lady'. The single-flowered *L. ×s.* 'Becky' is much taller, depending on soil and climate, reaching 90–150 cm (3–5 ft.), but is very popular for its ability to stay erect with a long flowering performance, and to withstand summer heat and humidity in North America. You either love or hate the doubles, whose heavier heads often flop after summer rains, but *L. ×s.* 'Aglaia' is a popular selection with fully fringed double petals and yellow centres, standing on 60-cm (2-ft.) stems, re-blooming if deadheaded. *L. ×s.* 'T.E. Killen', semi-double, and *L. ×s.* 'Wirral

Pride', large double, are old varieties, originally bred for cut flowers, both 60–90 cm (2–3 ft.) tall.

Liatris spicata 'Kobold'

gay feather, blazing star

This easy North American native displays striking poker-like heads of rich rose-purple flowers for weeks in summer.

L. spicata is the most commonly grown species and originates from eastern North America, from New Jersey in the north to Wisconsin in the west, south to Florida and Louisiana, growing in damp, open areas. It has a clumpy rootstock and stiff upright stems, 60–150 cm (2–5 ft.), with

Bold poker heads of rosy purple flowers of *Liatris spicata* 'Kobold' rise dramatically in front of the purple foliage of *Eupatorium rugosum* 'Chocolate' and *Crocosmia* 'Lucifer' behind in this grouping at Foggy Bottom.

→

Ligularia dentata 'Britt Marie Crawford' makes an imposing specimen plant in reasonably moist conditions.

flowers from purple and rose to white, the small flowers clasped on bottlebrush spikes opening from top to bottom over many weeks.

Good drainage is essential. Otherwise, any good garden soil that is not too dry, in sun or light shade, will produce good flowering displays. Undoubtedly the shorter-stemmed *L. s.* 'Kobold', a German selection meaning 'goblin', is excellent—and at only 60–75 cm (2–2½ ft.) it does not need staking. It has thick sturdy stems clothed with short, narrow dark green leaves and dense heads of rosy purple flowers, and like most *Liatris*, is excellent for cutting. In flower these are a magnet for bees and butterflies, and in autumn the seeds are enjoyed by birds, so stems should stay into winter. Once happy in appropriate conditions, *Liatris spicata* 'Kobold' and others in the genus are low maintenance, perhaps only needing to be divided in spring, when congested, every few years. Seedlings can be variable and disappointing, so ask for proven named cultivars.
60–75 cm (2–2½ ft.) × 30–45 cm (1–1½ ft.)
F mid to late summer
Z 3–9

Further Recommendations
A good white, with creamy flowers on 90-cm (3-ft.) spikes, is *L. s.* 'Floristan White'.

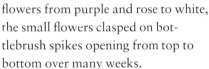

Ligularia dentata 'Britt Marie Crawford'

golden groundsel, bigleaf ligularia

This amazingly vibrant and dramatic moisture-loving plant has large glossy chocolate-brown leaves and contrasting orange-yellow flowers.

L. dentata 'Britt Marie Crawford' arose as a chance seedling, named after the lady in Scotland who spotted it but sadly died before she could enjoy its worldwide success. The species *L. dentata* is a native of China and Japan, growing in moist situations, in ditches, boggy areas and woodland clearings. It makes a mound of large kidney-shaped leaves and in midsummer yellow or golden daisy-like flowers appear above in clusters on upright stems. Some selections have been made with early purple leaves, most turning green later in summer with purple undersides—the popular and attractive *L. d.* 'Desdemona' and *L. d.*

'Othello', for instance—but *L. d.* 'Britt Marie Crawford' has put them all in the shade.

From early spring from a sturdy clumpy rootstock, small glossy chocolate-brown leaves with purple undersides begin to unfurl, forming mounds of overlapping shining foliage, unfortunately also much appreciated by slugs. Some may prefer to prevent the rather clashing orange-yellow flowers on purple spikes from blooming, although the result is eye-catching. These ligularias need a moist soil in sun or light shade in hotter climates, but too much shade will dull their colour. Ideal close to a water feature, pond or stream; in heat, leaves will flag if water is not available at the roots, although *L. d.* 'Britt Marie Crawford' seldom fades, and is more resistant to heat. Attractive seedheads follow in autumn, but if left, seeds freely germinate in moist conditions and can be a nuisance. If required, propagate any good named selection by division in early spring.
90–120 cm (3–4 ft.) × 75–90 cm (2½–3 ft.)
F mid to late summer
Z 3–8

→
The ground-covering lilyturf *Liriope muscari* thrives in this semi-shady setting, where it offers a real bonus in autumn with a display of purple flowers.

Liriope muscari

lilyturf

A lowly evergreen of quiet beauty, with late spikes of deep violet-blue to contrast with autumnal foliage of golds, browns and reds.

Liriope muscari is a clump-forming grass-like plant native to Korea, Japan and China where it grows in woods and clearings, gradually spreading, unlike the closely related *L. spicata*, which can be invasive given too much freedom (but makes excellent ground cover in shade).

L. muscari should have a place in every garden. It makes attractive dark green arching strap-like leaves in summer, followed by a good display of 30–45-cm (1–1½-ft.) purplish spikes whose small bright violet-purple buds open to bell-shaped flowers, the show lasting for weeks from late summer into autumn. With the protection of some shade in hotter climates and in milder localities, *L. muscari* is completely evergreen, but otherwise in extremes of heat, in open positions or in winter cold, the leaves will scorch. These should be trimmed back in spring to allow fresh new growth to begin another year. Liriopes require good drainage and once established they withstand dry conditions and drought, but plants will not flower so well in dense shade. It is excellent as an edging plant or beneath shrubs where not too dry or shady. Divide and plant if required in spring. There have been several named selections: *L. m.* 'Monroe White', with large clear white flowers, and *L. m.* 'Variegata', with yellow edged leaves and blue flowers, are both distinct. All grow more vigorously given the summer heat the species prefers.

30–45 cm (1–1½ ft.) × 30–45 cm (1–1½ ft.)

F late summer and autumn

Z 6–9

→
The golden-leaved ground cover *Luzula sylvatica* 'Aurea' holds its colour in winter and in shade, here flowering in early spring in Foggy Bottom with *Pulmonaria* 'Blue Ensign' behind.

Luzula sylvatica 'Aurea'

greater woodrush

This mat-forming ornamental grass is useful for its ability to grow in both moist and dry shade.

Luzula sylvatica is a European native, growing in moist and dry woodlands from Britain and western Europe across to the Caucasus. The species forms clumps of leathery evergreen leaves, covering the ground by spreading rhizomes, though it's seldom invasive. In spring it provides a display of greenish white flowers ageing to brown on 60-cm (2-ft.) stems.

Although they could hardly be described as spectacular, workman-like plants for difficult places can still be appreciated for their simple pleasures, and there is a place for them in most gardens. I rate the golden-yellow-leaved *L. s.* 'Aurea' for its ability to light up a shady area in summer or winter. It is a plant for shade or semi-shade, as in sun there is a tendency for leaves to scorch, but beneath a deciduous shrub or higher canopy evergreen it is effective, holding onto its colour well, particularly in winter. Although tolerant of shade and dry conditions, ensure spring or early planting of *Luzula* is followed by watering until established.

30–45 cm (1–1½ ft.) × 45–60 cm (1½–2 ft.)
F spring to early summer
Z 4–8

Further Recommendations

L. s. 'Marginata' (syn. *L. s.* 'Variegata') lightens the green with slim leaf margins of creamy white. Brighter are the creamy white-edged new leaves on *L. s.* 'Taggart's Cream', which tone down to green in summer. Consider the bright-green-leaved *L. nivea* too for its fine show of nearly white flowers on 60-cm (2-ft.) stems—a high-quality and easy plant where conditions are not too dry.

←

Caught here in the early morning light at Foggy Bottom in midsummer, the arching dew-laden leaves of *Miscanthus sinensis* 'Morning Light' are framed by *Geranium psilostemon* in the foreground and *Echinacea purpurea* behind.

Miscanthus sinensis 'Morning Light'

Japanese silver grass

Above all other miscanthus, *M. s.* 'Morning Light' is applauded for its grace, stature and ability to stand up to winter, remaining attractive longer than any other to date.

The species *M. sinensis* is native to mountainous and lowland areas throughout Japan, as well as China and Korea, forming clumps with grassy blades centred by a silvery white stripe. Reddish or silvery inflorescences on stems 90–240 cm (3–8 ft.) or taller occur in late summer. The foliage dies back in autumn, fading to straw colour and then greyish beige with considerable attraction in winter.

The main reason for growing *M. s.* 'Morning Light' (and most other variegated grasses) is for foliage, so if necessary flowering stems could be cut away before seed develops. *M. s.* 'Morning Light' was admired by the Japanese for years before it was 'discovered' in 1976 and brought to the U.S. National Arboretum in Washington, D.C., where it was later named *M. s.* 'Morning Light' by Kurt Bluemel. It forms a tight 120–150-cm (4–5-ft.) clump of narrow, erectly held light green leaves, finely margined with white. Similar in habit to the dark-green-leaved *M. s.* 'Gracillimus', it shares with it a shyness to flower in cooler summer climates. The plumes are relatively small and usually sparse, rather detracting from the gracefully outward-arching late summer leaves. In late autumn or early winter, depending on climate, growth dies back and leaves turn to brown then beige, standing up against wind and snowfall and continuing to contribute to the winter garden.

The foliage should be cut back to 10 cm (4 in.) in late winter or earlier if appearance is messy, using sharp secateurs or a powered hedge trimmer. In milder regions, if foliage is still green, cut back to 30 cm (1 ft.). Miscanthus will grow in most soils where not too dry and will normally be taller in moist fertile soils. *M. sinensis* cultivars make spreading clumps that eventually become thick and congested. A sharp spade in early spring will still need some effort to curb their outer basal growth, and even more effort may be required every few years to lift clumps and split, replanting with younger outside material. Older clumps are more inclined to flop after heavy rains or wind; during a long, wet growing season in Britain in 2007, this tendency was exacerbated in the plants' taller growth. Many dwarfer-growing forms are now available for smaller gardens, but in my view there should always be room for *M. s.* 'Morning Light'.

120–150 cm (4–5 ft.) × 90–120 cm (3–4 ft.)
F late summer to autumn, if at all
Z 5–9

Further Recommendations

Selection in Japan and the United States and breeding in Europe, notably by the late German breeder and nurseryman Ernst Pagels, has added to the variety of *Miscanthus* available, and in cooler climates it has also brought their flowering time forward from late autumn to late summer. The 100+ cultivars within *Miscanthus* are not without problems such as their freedom to disperse seed in warm climates, where there has been an unforeseen increase of self-seeding into native habitats, sometimes to the point of invasiveness; if you live in a hot area, seek advice before using *Miscanthus* species and cultivars.

Some view the size of *Miscanthus* as another drawback, but these ornamental grasses add a valuable sense of dimension to the garden, and although few small or medium gardens will be able to accommodate them, taller selections have a place in larger borders and landscapes. Among them are *M. s.* 'Malepartus', with reddish purple plumes turning to silver, and fairly broad leaves, 240 cm (8 ft.)

tall, and *M. s.* 'Zwergelefant' ('Dwarf Elephant'), similar but with curiously twisted unfurling purple-red inflorescences, 180 cm (6 ft.) tall. Somewhat finer and lower is *M. s.* 'Flamingo', with narrow leaves, graceful foliage and delicate-looking reddish pink plumes that turn silver, 150–180 cm (5–6 ft.) high. *M. s.* 'Kaskade', one of the most attractive with large pendulous rose-pink plumes on wavy stems

held well above the foliage, needs an open position and is 150 cm (5 ft.) tall. *M. s.* 'Ferner Osten' ('Far East') is excellent for the smaller garden, similar to *M. s.* 'Flamingo' but reaching at maximum 120–150 cm (4–5 ft.). Still going down in height, with green leaves thinly banded white, consider *M. s.* 'Yaku Jima', with narrow leaves and masses of small silver plumes, vase-shaped, 120–150 cm (4–5 ft.) and

←
Growing from beneath the ground in early spring to 240 cm (8 ft.) or more in height by late summer, *Miscanthus* provides structure and displays colourful and changing plumage. Lower contrasting perennials such as *Geranium* 'Rozanne' accentuate its stature. The plant with variegated foliage in the centre is *Arundo donax* var. *versicolor*, while the miscanthus, right centre, is *M. s.* 'Ferner Osten'.

M. s. 'Little Kitten', with longer stems and plumes, but only 80–120 cm (3–4 ft.) overall.

In some respects you get a longer period of interest from miscanthus with variegated foliage, but many tend to flop later in the season. *M. s.* 'Strictus', 180 cm (6 ft.), with its upright habit, has mid green leaves interrupted by irregular bands of horizontal yellow stripes. New but not widely proven is the dwarfer zebra grass, *M. s.* 'Gold Bar', with bright golden bands on green leaves to 90–120 cm (3–4 ft.). *M. s.* 'Morning Light' stands alone for its narrow variegated leaves, but among broader-leaved cultivars *M. s.* 'Variegatus', 150–180 cm (5–6 ft.) high with broad white stripes on green leaves, is the most widely used but has a tendency to flop as it gets older, and although shorter and more compact, *M. s.* 'Dixieland', 120–150 cm (4–5 ft.), can be similarly prone. Regular division and avoiding overcrowding may help. Both make striking specimens. All are excellent for flower-arranging. **Z** 5–9.

Molinia caerulea 'Variegata'

purple moor grass

A still-underused and underrated ornamental grass, *M. c.* 'Variegata' is noteworthy for its almost-year-round appeal in foliage and flower.

Green-leaved *M. caerulea* is native to a huge area of Britain and to most of Europe across to eastern Asia, where it grows on mainly acid soils, peaty or sandy heathlands and mountainous regions. Until recently shorter selections, flowering less than 90 cm (3 ft.) high, were considered distinct from the taller and larger forms which, although inflorescences are light and airy, can reach 240 cm (8 ft.), these formerly being grouped under the unwieldy name of *Molinia caerulea* subsp. *arundinacea*. Now the differences are seen as cultural, so unusually the taxonomists and botanists have made our life simpler and all cultivars are seen as selections of *M. caerulea*, although it may take some time for books and catalogues to catch up.

All are clump-forming grasses, with narrow, sharply pointed leaves well below the erect or arching stems which bear mostly purple-tinted inflorescences that turn to gold on ripening, leaves and flowers becoming golden-orange depending on situation, through late autumn and early winter. *M. c.* 'Variegata' is suitable for any size of garden with creamy yellow to bright yellow striped leaves forming a neat mound of arching foliage and a free display of greenish yellow flowers to 75 cm (2½ ft.) in late summer. The foliage will be brighter in full sun and in drier conditions, but the majority of molinias including *M. c.* 'Variegata' grow well on most soils

In late summer, *Molinia caerulea* 'Variegata' makes a graceful foliage and flowering foreground to enhance various perennials in Foggy Bottom.

these were introduced by German plantsmen who fully appreciate their native grasses. Both reach 60–90 cm (2–3 ft.). Among the taller cultivars are molinias with open and widely arching inflorescences held well above the foliage that can be seen through at eye level—graceful, with delicate traceries of flowers transformed by wind, dew or early frost. *M. c.* 'Transparent' spreads more widely than *M. c.* 'Zuneigung', both with flowers reaching 180 cm (6 ft.). These are best planted as specimens, while those of a more upright habit, such as *M. c.* 'Karl Foerster', 180–210 cm (6–7 ft.) high, and the spectacular *M. c.* 'Skyracer' (well named by selector Kurt Bluemel), narrowly erect to 240 cm (8 ft.), work well in groups or as repeated accent plants. All **Z** 4–8.

Monarda didyma 'Gardenview Scarlet'

beebalm, bergamot, oswego tea

One of the best beebalms, *M. d.* 'Gardenview Scarlet' has an erect habit, intense glowing scarlet flowers loved by bees and butterflies, and good mildew resistance.

and are reasonably drought-tolerant. Their origins indicate a preference for cooler temperate climates, being less successful in hotter summer regions. The shorter-flowered cultivars remain attractive through winter and flower stems stand up well, but the taller types, magnificent in autumn, are prone to collapse in early winter after the first gales or early snowfall. Cut back to the clump when this happens and the shorter forms in spring. Division and planting is best in early spring

from a rather woody rootstock.
45–60 cm (1½–2 ft.) × 45–60 cm (1½–2 ft.)
F late summer to winter
Z 4–8

Further Recommendations
For the smaller garden, in addition to *M. c.* 'Variegata' consider the slender arching spikes and flowers of *M. c.* 'Strahlenquelle', or the narrow, densely erect stems of *M. c.* 'Moorhexe'; like so many others,

→
Few perennials make more impact than some of the beebalms at their summer peak, en masse or close up. *Monarda didyma* 'Gardenview Scarlet' is striking with the white-headed *Hydrangea arborescens* 'Annabelle' behind, in Adrian's Wood at Bressingham.

The two main ornamental species of this aromatic perennial originate from eastern North America. *Monarda didyma*, oswego tea, grows in light, moist woodland along edges of lakes and waterways, forming spreading mats of roots and basal leaves, *M. fistulosa*, the wild bergamot, also a woodland-edge-lover, is more clump-forming and grows in drier situations. The latter is less prone to powdery mildew, but in reality many of the most attractive and gardenworthy cultivars come of mixed parentage and can only be judged on performance.

M. 'Gardenview Scarlet' was selected some years ago by Henry Ross, plantsman and owner of Gardenview Horticultural Park in Cleveland, Ohio and is an outstanding cultivar. It is a vigorous plant with square erect stems bearing bright green lance-shaped, incised leaves, topped in midsummer by reddish bracts beneath cone-like heads from which emerge bright scarlet tubular flowers that are aromatic when rubbed. Best in part shade or full sun in cooler summer climates, it needs more shade and moisture in hotter regions. Although *M.* 'Gardenview Scarlet' and others mentioned here are sometimes described as mildew-resistant, mildew still may appear later in summer as flowering finishes, or under drier conditions. If unsightly, cut all foliage down to 15 cm (6 in.) and dispose of it.

Monardas are usually worth some trouble in maintenance, so spreading mats may need curbing in spring and dead central patches will need filling; consider lifting and replanting with young material, having dug over and composted the soil first, perhaps every three years. Good air circulation helps, so even thinning bushy plants by removing a few stems may be worthwhile. In cooler climates and moist conditions, some plants may get taller than books or catalogues state. Cutting new growth back by a third in late spring when growth is 60 cm (2 ft.) will keep plants more compact, although it will delay flowering. The often-vibrant colours and unusual flowers really add a unique ingredient to the summer garden where the right conditions can be met.

120–150 cm (4–5 ft.) × 60–75 cm (2–2½ ft.)

F mid to late summer

Z 4–8

Further Recommendations

Similar, slightly shorter and less erect is the scarlet-red *M.* 'Jacob Cline', and for a mildew-resistant pink *M.* 'Marshall's Delight' has not been bettered—both 90–120 cm (3–4 ft.). At this same height is an old German cultivar, *M.* 'Blaustrumpf' ('Blue Stocking'), which is hardly blue—but its deep violet-purple flowers are a great contrast to yellow rudbeckias in summer, and although tall, the recent introduction, long-flowering *M.* 'Raspberry Wine', 120–150 cm (4–5 ft.), with deep wine-red flow-

ers, is already a favourite of mine. Lastly, *M.* 'Violet Queen' is a good performer, with rather open foliage to 120 cm (4 ft.) and a good display of soft violet flowers. All of these are mildew-resistant.

Nepeta racemosa 'Walker's Low'

catmint

Knitting the early summer border together, this tough, aromatic perennial is excellent for many uses, and attractive in its own right.

The most common and well-loved catmints are mostly sun-loving aromatic perennials, originating from southern Europe across to the Caucasus. *N. racemosa* (syn. *N. mussinii*),

which grows in stony, well-drained open areas, is a variable plant, as many species are in nature, reaching 30–75 cm (1–2½ ft.), with grey-green leaves and light to deep blue and violet flowers.

Initially, *N. r.* 'Walker's Low' may have sold due to its somewhat misleading name, rather than its performance; it is not actually low-growing, but rather came from Walker's Low Nursery in England. Regardless, it has proven to be a great performer as a garden plant when conditions permit. Reaching 60–90 cm (2–3 ft.), it has soft grey-green leaves and an abundance of broadly upright and spreading spikes with a mass of lavender-blue flowers from early to late summer. It prefers an open, sunny position with

←
Nepeta racemosa 'Walker's Low' provides the first early summer flowers above the leaves of *Hakonechloa macra* 'Albovariegata' in a rather dry semi-shady position in Foggy Bottom.

good drainage, and is adaptable to light shade and more general soils although, like most of these nepetas, it dislikes winter wet. When flowers become sparser in mid to late summer, trim back the foliage by two thirds to tidy up and get a renewed flowering into autumn. Propagation is best by division in spring, and early cuttings soon root in spring or on new growth following trimming in late summer.

Cats of course like the aromatic catmint and enjoy rolling in the foliage, which may be all right if you like your cat more than your catmint. If you do not, take the advice of a respected plantsman, the late Graham Stuart Thomas, who suggested putting some twigs of thorny *Berberis* or a rose among the foliage as a deterrent. However, in my experience cats are less likely to trouble *N. r.* 'Walker's Low' than *N. ×faasenii*, a popular, dwarfer catmint to 45–60 cm (1½–2ft.) with lighter blue flowers, or the robust *N.* 'Six Hills Giant', a hybrid with larger leaves, strong 90-cm (3-ft.) stems and deeper violet blue flowers. All are excellent to mix in foreground plantings, their foliage and flowers spreading much more widely than their clumpy rootstock, blending

effortlessly with achilleas, peonies, roses and many more summer-flowering plants.
60–90 cm (2–3 ft.) × 90–120 cm (3–4 ft.)
F early to late summer
Z 3–8

Ophiopogon planiscapus 'Nigrescens'

black mondo grass, dwarf lilyturf

The more I use it, the more I value this black-leaved evergreen grass-like plant, its foliage unique for creating dramatic associations.

The green-leaved mondo grass, *Ophiopogon planiscapus*, is native to the main Japanese island of Honshu, as well as Shikoku and Kyushu, mostly growing in shady woodland or woodland edges and clearings. It has a slowly spreading habit with narrow dark green strap-like leaves to 15–20 cm (6–8 in.) and a sparse display of small white flowers in summer on 20–30-cm (8–12-in.) stems. It is an unremarkable, rather dull plant. You might then consider a black-leaved version to be even duller, but quite the contrary.

Whoever in Japan first discovered *O. p.* 'Nigrescens' discovered a 'black gold' plant for gardeners. This plant is similar to the species in form and habit, but has glossy black leaves, a denser habit and racemes of purple-tinted flowers on narrow black stems producing black rounded fruits by autumn. It is a dramatic plant and also, in North America particularly, has been given the descriptive names of 'Black Dragon' and 'Ebony Knight'. For best results it needs to be given a reasonable, moisture-retentive soil, in sun or shade, as it will be a shadow of itself in too dry a position, with leaves browning and shrivelling. On light soils it may spread more thinly, so add compost before planting and mulch. Treat similarly on heavy clay soils, so that slowly spreading stolons can increase this valuable mat-forming plant. Established clumps can be lifted or curbed in spring if required so runners or divisions can be planted elsewhere, firming wiry roots and watering in well. The black fruits sown outdoors in autumn will produce about 60% black- and 40% green-leaved seedlings in spring.

O. p. 'Nigrescens' has a multitude of uses. Try it beneath deciduous shrubs

 A winter frost adds a lightening touch to the jet-black evergreen leaves of *Ophiopogon planiscapus* 'Nigrescens'.

→

In the Summer Garden at Bressingham, clumps of erect steel-blue foliage of *Panicum virgatum* 'Northwind' contrast with flat-headed *Sedum* 'Matrona', just coming into flower in late summer.

Five months later, in late winter, the same combination is still providing excellent garden value, both plants having died back but holding up against the winter weather. ↘

or high canopy evergreens, with variegated or golden-leaved hostas or the silver-patterned *Brunnera macrophylla* 'Jack Frost'. It is particularly stunning with *Hakonechloa macra* 'Alboaurea'.

15–25 cm (6–10 in.) × 30–45 cm (1–1½ ft.) and spreading
F late summer, black fruits in autumn
Z 6–10

Panicum virgatum 'Northwind'

switch grass

A tough and reliable ornamental grass whose erect steel-blue foliage and ability to withstand wind and snow as it changes colour through summer, autumn and winter can rival any miscanthus.

P. v. 'Northwind', selected and named by Roy Diblik of Northwind Perennial Farm in Wisconsin, is one of many selections of the North American switch grass adding to the palette of ornamental grasses available to gardeners. The species is widespread through much of the North American continent, from Nova Scotia west to

→
Fluffy inflorescences of *Pennisetum orientale* arch gracefully on a summer morning in Foggy Bottom.

Manitoba and south to Arizona and Mexico, Florida and even the islands of the Caribbean where it grows in open landscapes and prairies and on woodland edges. It prefers full sun, is drought-tolerant once established, and will also grow in boggy areas.

Is this, then, the perfectly adaptable plant? *P. v.* 'Northwind' comes close, as its 150–180-cm (5–6-ft.) foliage stays erect during summer and winter, while that of many other selections with weaker stems flops all too easily before summer is through. It has deep steel-blue-green, narrow, pointed leaves that turn a light gold in autumn and pink-tinted, airy inflorescences tucked in close to the foliage in late summer. It is resistant to rust in hot to humid regions. *P. v.* 'Northwind' and other cultivars are clump-forming, slowly increasing with age. Large plants can be curbed in early spring after cutting back the previous year's foliage, and can be propagated by division in the same way as *Miscanthus* with which it shares similar uses, its tolerance of dry conditions a definite advantage.

150–180 cm (5–6 ft.) × 90 cm (3 ft.)

F late summer

Z 4–9

Further Recommendations

P. v. 'Heavy Metal' with grey-blue leaves and a more open, upright form to 150 cm (5 ft.) is also a good choice for its ability to stand up against all weathers, and for its drought tolerance and flowering performance. Some cultivars have crimson- or reddish-tinged foliage, although this is seldom consistent throughout the plant and may vary according to location and climate. German selections *P. v.* 'Hänse Herms', *P. v.* 'Rehbraun' and *P. v.* 'Rotstrahlbusch', all 90–120 cm (3–4 ft.) high, all have delicate cloudy inflorescences and red-to-purple-tipped or -suffused foliage, and *P. v.* 'Shenandoah', 120 cm (4 ft.) high, selected from seedlings of *P .v.* 'Hänse Herms' by German plantsman Hans Simon, has some of the most intense wine-red leaves of all, though this leaf colouration seldom occurs before late summer.

Pennisetum orientale

Oriental fountain grass

From early summer to early winter this beautiful grass adds form, grace and movement gardens of all sizes.

This sun-loving ornamental grass is native to North Africa, Saudi Arabia, Turkey, Iran and the Caucasus to northwest India, growing in open rocky areas, screes and hillsides. It forms a clump of narrow green leaves, and erupts into bloom with hairy purplish bottlebrush heads arching gracefully on 60–75-cm (2–2½-ft.) stems from midsummer, earlier in hotter regions. These fade to off-white, then beige, and the foliage also has autumnal tones of gold, then brown. Given its origins, *P. orientale* needs sun, or part shade in warm climates, and good drainage. The flowers and foliage tend to collapse by midwinter, but can be left until it looks scruffy or to early spring before cutting back. It can be raised from seed, and established clumps can be lifted and divided in spring for replanting.

60–75 cm (2–2½ ft.) × 45–60 cm (1½–2 ft.)

F midsummer to autumn

Z 6–9

Further Recommendations

The species *P. orientale* seldom varies, but *P. o.* 'Karley Rose' was selected for its greater hardiness (**Z** 5–9) and deep rose-pink heads on 90-cm (3-ft.) stems.

green leaves and green-tinged flowers changing to creamy white, 60–75 cm (2–2½ ft.). *P. a.* 'Little Bunny' is a charming miniature, with compact clumps of narrow dark green leaves producing small heads of creamy white flowers on 30–45-cm (1–1½-ft.) stems in late summer. Quite different, striking with broad deep green glossy arching leaves and dark purple-black flowerheads, is the black fountain grass, *P. a.* 'Moudry'. Autumn-flowering even in warmer regions, it unfortunately seldom flowers in cooler temperate areas. 75–90 cm (2½–3 ft.) high. Cut all back in spring.

Persicaria amplexicaulis 'Taurus'

red bistort, knotweed

Less widely used than it should be, *P. a.* 'Taurus' has broad leafy green foliage and crimson flower spikes from midsummer to autumn frosts.

Although the dreaded Japanese knotweed has had its name changed from *Polygonum* (now *Persicaria*) to *Fallopia japonica*, its reputation nonetheless continues to affect that of other knotweeds, among which there are some unruly or invasive plants but

Although some of the many cultivars of *Pennisetum alopecuroides* tend to either be shy to flower, or flower too late to make an impact in cooler temperate regions, they are mostly robust, hardy and capable of making a great impact in the late summer and autumn garden. It is a variable species growing in sun in lowland areas in Japan and southeastern Asia, clump-forming with green summer leaves turning gold then beige in autumn and winter, the bottlebrush spikes held stiffly in and above the foliage. One of the most popular selections, raised in Germany, is the compact *P. a.* 'Hameln' with

←

Autumn afternoon sun enhances the late deep scarlet flowers of *Persicaria amplexicaulis* 'Taurus'.

also some valuable, gardenworthy ones.

P. amplexicaulis is native to Afghanistan across to western China, growing in scrub and moist alpine meadows and streamsides at high altitudes, and has produced some good garden plants, none better in my view than *P. a.* 'Taurus'.

P. a. 'Taurus' arose at Bressingham as a seedling from *P. a.* 'Firetail', an earlier selection made by Alan Bloom, with scarlet flowers clustered around poker-like spikes to 120 cm (4 ft.). *P. a.* 'Taurus', introduced in 1985, has a more compact habit, making a leafy mound of rich green oval, pointed leaves from which emerge a succession of large, deep crimson bottlebrush flowers from midsummer until autumn frosts. Although hardy (Z 4–9), a sharp frost will quickly collapse the abundant foliage, which can be cut away when unsightly. *Persicaria amplexicaulis* has a woody rootstock and a spreading but noninvasive habit, likely to be more vigorous in moist soils, but growing surprisingly well in drier situations. Any spreading can be curbed in spring, when plants can be lifted and divided. Best in sun or light shade. Because it is vigorous and makes a lot of foliage, it is not easy to handle in containers, so is not seen widely on garden centres—a pity, since this perennial has considerable merit. 75–90 cm (2½–3 ft.) × 90–120 cm (3–4 ft.)
F midsummer to late autumn
Z 4–9

Further Recommendations

White and pink forms of *P. a.* 'Taurus' can be found in *P. a.* 'Alba' and 'Rosea' respectively, both 90 cm (3 ft.) high.

P. bistorta 'Superbum', a selection from the common bistort, is native to moist locations and mountain meadows across much of Europe and eastern Asia and is on the invasive side, but with its showy spring performance it is worth considering for its broad, pointed mid green leaves and softest-pink bottlebrush spikes to 90 cm (3 ft.). It prefers an average to moist situation in sun or light shade and can be curbed each spring. *P. b.* 'Hohe Tatra' may be a better choice, clump-forming with dark green leaves and flower buds a bright cherry red, opening to deep pink, best in a moist soil, 60–75 cm (2–2½ ft.) high. Both **Z** 4–9.

For the larger garden or landscape, a relatively recent introduction from the Himalayas, the enormous *P. polymorphum*, is nothing short of spectacular. Clump-forming but liable to seed, it makes an impressive vase-shaped bush of dense foliage topped by large panicles of white flowers, lasting for weeks from midsummer, later still attractive with autumnal hues of rose-pink, then brown, in sun or light shade sheltered from strong winds, on moist to average soil. 180–240 cm (6–8 ft.) × 150–190 cm (5–6 ft.), **Z** 5–9.

Phlox paniculata 'Franz Schubert'

border phlox, summer phlox

This cultivar is a worthy representative of the indispensable border phlox: healthy, mildew-resistant and with heads of soft-lilac-tinged pink flowers, it gives colour and fragrance to high summer.

Most species of *Phlox* are native to North America, some spring-flowering woodland perennials and others sun-loving ground-coverers. *P. paniculata*, which grows to 60–150 cm (2–5 ft.) in the wild, can be found in the eastern states from New York in the north,

west to Ohio, and south to Louisiana growing in light or open woodland, along water courses, in scrub and on hillsides. From the earliest introduction of the species to Europe in 1730, considerable breeding work, particularly in England and Germany, led to a proliferation of cultivars coloured white, pink, orange, red, purple and almost-blue, with many shades or contrasts within individual flowers. Small heads, large flowers; large heads, small flowers: all are fragrant, but some more so than others.

As many pass into history, many more new selections arrive—bred for flowering performance, compact and dwarfer habit and above all mildew resistance. These will need to be given the test of time across many locations, but there is a general consensus among expert horticultural observers as to the most mildew resistance, this term applied since even the resistant cultivars can in certain conditions, heat, and particularly drought be susceptible to mildew late in the season. Since *P. p.* 'Franz Schubert' was selected by my father at Bressingham in 1980 and named after his favourite composer,

←

Phlox paniculata 'Franz Schubert' is seen here in the Dell Garden in late summer with *Helenium* 'Waltraut'.

it has travelled and performed well across the world, the pastel soft lilac flowers held on terminal clusters or panicles on erect 90–120-cm (3–4-ft.) stems from late midsummer until early autumn.

Phlox paniculata cultivars are clump-forming, with spreading but not invasive roots, the woody stems clothed in lance-shaped leaves, which depending on the cultivar may be green, purple or bronze-tinged, and variegated. Best in a good organic soil that does not dry out, with good drainage in winter, full sun or part shade. For mildew prevention, never guaranteed, do not overcrowd with neighbouring plants, and thin congested stems by midsummer to help create good air circulation. If mildew is a serious problem, cut plants to the ground and discard, but do not compost stems. Phlox are heavy feeders and roots will become congested after three or four years, so in early spring, lift, divide with two forks, discard old woody material and replant in soil enriched with moisture-retaining compost using younger outside divisions. In some climates seeding can be a problem in which case cut back flowers when finished. In other cooler or wetter climates, taller cultivars can be reduced in height by pruning back new growth in late spring or early summer by half, which reduces height but as always results in slightly smaller and later flowers.

120–150 cm (4–5 ft.) × 45–60 cm (1½–2 ft.)

F mid to late summer

Z 4–9

Further Recommendations

There may be others, but the recognized mildew-resistant cultivars include: *P. p.* 'Bright Eyes' with pink flowers and a deep red eye, 90 cm (3 ft.) high; *P. p.* 'David' with glossy green leaves and pure white flowers, 120–150 cm (4–5 ft.); *P. p.* 'Eva Cullum' with an erect habit and dark green leaves, with a rose-pink, crimson eye, 120–150 cm (4–5 ft.); *P. p.* 'Flamingo' with large panicles and a soft pink with red centre, 90–120 cm (3–4 ft.); *P. p.* 'Norah Leigh', strong-growing for a variegated form, with pale green leaves irregularly edged with creamy white, and small pink flowers, 75–90 cm (2½–3 ft.); *P. p.* 'Prince of Orange' (syn. *P. p.* 'Orange') with orange-red flowers, difficult to place, 60–90 cm (2–3 ft); *P. p.* 'The King' with strong violet-red flowers, 90–120 cm (3–4 ft.); and the more recent *P. p.* 'Blue Paradise', 75–90 cm (2½–3 ft.), whose purple-blue colour changes with the light, though even then it is seldom true blue.

Many more excellent cultivars exist, and if mildew is seldom a problem in your garden the choice is endless. Although dwarfer cultivars may be attractive in containers and convenient

←

Flowering in midsummer, *Phlox maculata* 'Natascha' will brighten up any garden.

Alan Bloom selected a seedling from *P. m.* 'Alpha' with a sturdy habit, its white flowers centred red and introduced it in 1966 under the name *P. m.* 'Omega', but perhaps most striking of all is the selection *P. m.* 'Natascha', found as a sport in the Minsk Botanic Garden around 1990, with startling bicoloured petals, white overlayed by pink like the spokes of a wheel: perhaps not natural, but still a wonder of nature.

Polygonatum ×hybridum 'Striatum'

variegated Solomon's seal

This variegated Solomon's seal will brighten up any shady spot—useful, attractive and succeeding in dry soil once established.

The showiest of the variegated leaf forms, *Polygonatum ×hybridum* 'Striatum' is an excellent woodland plant, robust in habit and able to brighten up any shady spot. It arose as a sport on the wavy, green lance-shaped-leaved *P.* ×hybridum, a natural cross between *P. odoratum* and *P. multiflorum*, both native to Europe to Asia where they grow in woods

for plants sold in flower at garden centres, in my opinion those 90 cm (3 ft.) or higher fit better with planting schemes among other perennials and grasses.

Phlox maculata, the early phlox or meadow phlox, and its cultivars are gardenworthy perennials, similar in origin to *P. paniculata* and its requirements for good soil with reasonable moisture. They quickly make dense clumps with many erectly held stems with glossy slender green leaves, the fragrant flowers held on cylindrical clusters in early summer. All cultivars are highly resistant to mildew, and congested clumps will need dividing every two or three years in soil enriched by compost. There are few cultivars in a limited colour range, all 90–120 cm (3–4 ft.). **Z** 3–9.

P. m. 'Alpha' was raised by renowned German nurseryman and breeder Georg Arends in 1912 and has dark green stems and leaves and heads of soft lilac-pink flowers. Similar but deeper in colour is *P. m.* 'Rosalinde'.

→

Growing well once established, even in dry shade, *Polygonatum ×hybridum* 'Striatum' is a cool plant both for flowers in spring and brightly variegated foliage.

and shady areas. This hybrid has a fleshy creeping rootstock, late to produce sturdy gently arching stems with glossy green undulating leaves, beneath which in early summer hang clusters of small creamy white green-tipped bell-like flowers spaced along the stem, and blue fruits in autumn. It is a graceful plant, the variegated form *P. ×h.* 'Striatum' similar in all respects except that the leaves are brushed irregularly with creamy white striations, both making summer-long dense foliage cover to 75 cm (2½ ft.), the leaves turning gold or yellow in the autumn. Expect occasional reversion to green leaves on some plants. Plants prefer good organic soil, and although slow to establish, particularly from open-ground divided plants, once they have done so they will spread happily, even into very dry soil in shade. Low-maintenance, the roots can become congested after many years, and if the display is affected, or the spread needs curbing, lift and carefully divide, replanting in early spring. Old groups can be mulched with leaf mould in winter after cutting down the previous year's foliage. Although generally pest-free, watch out for spring slug activity and in early summer for sawfly larvae

or caterpillars, which can strip the foliage in a matter of days.

There has long been some confusion in the naming of many polygonatums. *P. hybridum* 'Striatum' was previously listed under *P. multiflorum* 'Variegatum', and the attractively but more subtly variegated-leaved *P. odoratum* var. *pluriflorum* 'Variegatum' from Japan was (and still is in some publications) listed under *P. falcatum* 'Variegatum'. This form has reddish stems, 60–75 cm (2–2½ ft.) high, lighter

green leaves thinly edged with cream, and pendulous slightly fragrant flowers smaller than *P. ×hybridum* with small blue-black fruits in autumn. Given its Japanese origins, it is not surprising that this form is particularly heat-tolerant.

60–90 cm (2–3 ft.) × 45–60 cm (1½–2 ft.), spreading
F early summer
Z 4–9

mulching; apart from seed, this is the best way to reproduce. The origins of *P. vulgaris* indicate its versatility and give a clue to where it will succeed, which includes moist meadows. Often in hot, drier situations plants will go dormant to reappear next late winter or early spring, but in hotter regions in particular shade will be necessary. It is only fair to point out that while the English primrose is a beautiful spring plant, it is not without potential problems. It doesn't favour light sandy soils, nor will it thrive in badly drained situations. Pests such as aphids, weevils, mites and nematodes are mentioned but these are more likely with some of the hybrids and in nursery production situations.

15 cm (6 in.) × 15–30 cm (½–1 ft.)
F late winter to spring
Z 4–9

Further Recommendations

I also highly rate the bright lilac-pink- and occasionally white-flowered *P. v.* subsp. *sibthorpii* which originates from Greece, Turkey to the Caucasus. It is the same size as *P. vulgaris*, favours similar conditions and should be cultivated and reproduced in the same way.

Primula vulgaris

primrose, English primrose

The common primrose is an indispensable part of the spring garden, cheerful and seeding freely in the heavier soils it prefers.

The mostly evergreen common primrose is a plant for scattering in various places in the garden, beside pathways, beneath deciduous shrubs and trees, ideally on heavier soil that retains some moisture in summer. The species in the wild is spread across western Europe from the British Isles to Ukraine, Turkey and even northwestern Africa. It grows in woodland, alpine meadows and shady rocky areas. In Foggy Bottom it grows and seeds close to tree roots in heavy soil that dries in summer, the early spring flowers pale 'primrose'-yellow to cream with considerable variation in petal size.

Where happy, it will make clumps that will live for years although older plants can be divided immediately after flowering has finished, trimming off the leaves, watering, firming and

Pulmonaria 'Diana Clare'

lungwort

This cultivar, one among so many invaluable lungworts, is vigorous, showy in flower for weeks in spring and continues as a dramatic foliage plant right into winter.

In recent years there has been an explosion of interest in this group of spring flowering and foliage plants, fed partly by the ease with which new hybrid seedlings have arisen in gardens, and a growing realization by gardeners of their versatility and worthiness. The 15 or so species originate from western to eastern Europe, some edging into Russia and Siberia. Many grow in sun or shade in alpine regions where not too dry, and are generally clump-forming with hairy leaves, rough to the touch, with clusters of bell-shaped flowers from early spring to early summer. Many of the species are valuable garden plants, but have largely been surpassed by some superb hybrids among the 200 or so forms in cultivation.

↑
Later in summer, after cutting back spent flowers, a long display is given by the silver-grey leaves of *Pulmonaria* 'Diana Clare', next to *Hosta* 'Shade Fanfare' and the deep purple foliage of *Heuchera* 'Obsidian'.

Despite competition from some somewhat similar cultivars, *P.* 'Diana Clare', selected by English plantsman Bob Brown and named for his wife, has become an acknowledged favourite. With a long display of blue flowers, ageing to violet, followed by

→

Its bronzed, ribbed and cut leaves make moisture-loving *Rodgersia podophylla* a fine foliage plant, seen here in mid spring.

large, long pointed silvery leaves, this is a long-interest plant with many uses.

Pulmonarias are hardy and indispensable in the garden, in my view, and for cooler temperate climates they are easily grown given sun or half shade where neither too dry nor too wet. In hotter regions, shade and some moisture will be necessary; these are ideal plants for light woodland, shady path edges, beneath roses and other deciduous shrubs. Where happy, some species and cultivars seed rather freely although they will differ from the parent and each other, and unless striking are probably best removed. Sprawling, spent flowers and stems and old leaves should be cut back immediately after flowering particularly on good foliage forms to allow fresh leaves to develop, and if dry, water well at this time to encourage new growth. In damper or more humid climates mildew can be a problem on some cultivars; infected leaves should be pruned to the base and disposed of. Propagation, when necessary, is by division, either after spring flowering or, as I prefer, in early autumn, cutting back at least two thirds of foliage and then dividing and replanting the youngest, best-rooted material. Water in well.

30–45 cm (1–1½ ft.) × 45–60 cm (1½–2 ft.)
F spring
Z 4–8

Further Recommendations

P. 'Blue Ensign', clump-forming, is one of the earliest to flower, with strong deep blue flowers and dark green leaves, 30 cm (1 ft.) × 45 cm (1½ ft.). I also recommend *P.* 'Lewis Palmer' (syn. *P.* 'Highdown'), free-flowering and vigorous with dark green leaves spotted silvery white and violet-blue flowers; *P. longifolia* 'Bertram Anderson', with a neat clump of long slender green leaves spotted with silver, and bright blue flowers. A seedling of 'Bertram Anderson', *P.* 'Roy Davidson', has a similar habit and leaves, but light blue flowers. *P.* 'Opal', an excellent foliage plant with mounds of mid green spotted foliage and a free display of pale blue flowers, is one of the latest in bloom. All 30–45 cm (1–1½ ft.) × 45 cm (1½ ft.).

P. rubra 'Redstart', with light green unspotted leaves and a long display of soft red flowers in spring, needs some moisture to be at its best. *P. saccharata* 'Leopard', with striking dark green leaves contrasting with silver spots

and deep red flowers that fade to lilac, is excellent. Both 30 cm (1 ft.) × 30 cm (1 ft), spring-flowering, **Z** 4–8.

Rodgersia podophylla

Rodger's flower

For those with a moist spot, this handsome-leaved perennial adds stature to the spring and summer garden.

Recent selection and breeding has added even more impact to flower and foliage than that provided by the original seven or so species of these large-leaved, moisture-loving perennials from Asia. *R. podophylla* is a native of Japan and Korea, growing in mountain regions in moist woods and valleys. From a stout clump come creeping rhizomes, late in spring to shoot, but quickly developing large bronze-purple leaves on 90–120-cm (3–4-ft.) stems. Each is 30–40 cm (1–1⅓ ft.) in diameter, made up of five duck-foot-shaped leaflets that turn green in summer, and in sunnier positions *R. podophylla* has attractive red autumn tints on the foliage; 150-cm (5-ft.) spikes holding clusters of white flowers appear, usually sparsely, in summer above the leaf canopy.

→
Rudbeckia fulgida var. *sullivantii* 'Goldsturm' looks very natural here in Foggy Bottom with fellow American native *Eupatorium maculatum*. On the left is *Stipa gigantea*, with *Phlox paniculata* 'Franz Schubert' behind.

In cooler temperate climates, *R. podophylla* and other rodgersias will grow in sun or shade given reasonable moisture but shade is necessary as well as constant moisture in hotter summer regions; otherwise leaves are prone to scorch or desiccation. Rodgersias generally dislike waterlogging or too much winter wet, but where they can be grown they have a considerable presence. Although noninvasive, where happy *R. podophylla* may spread and need curbing with a spade as new growth appears in spring, which is also the best time to divide and replant, although this can also be done in autumn. Early growth can be caught by spring frosts. Damaged leaves and stems should be removed and new growth will recover. Once autumn frosts have started, the rodgersias usually begin to collapse and can be cut back.
120–150 cm (4–5 ft.) × 90–120 cm (3–4 ft.)
F summer
Z 5–8

Further Recommendations

It is worth adding further choices and comments to the list of recommended rodgersias because some species and cultivars are relatively easily grown and undeniably spectacular, even if they can be slow to establish. The following need some shade and moisture, the amount depending on climate. *R. aesculifolia* var. *henricii* is a non-spreading clump-former whose seven horse-chestnut-shaped leaves are bronzed on early growth, followed by heads of tightly bunched pink flowers, deepening to red, striking all through summer. 120–150 cm (4–5 ft.) × 75–120 cm (2½–4 ft.).

R. pinnata 'Superba' is a selection of the white- or pink-flowered species from western China with narrow glossy green, ribbed leaves on red stems, and spikes of deep pink flowers. Foliage and flowers deepen in colour in late summer, giving a long season of interest. Several recent cultivars, *R. p.* 'Crug Cardinal', *R. p.* 'Chocolate Wing' and *R. p.* 'Buckland Beauty', are worth looking out for as they become available more quickly through micropropagation. All 90–120 cm (3–4 ft.) × 60–90 cm (2–3 ft.), **F** summer, **Z** 5–8.

Rudbeckia fulgida var. *sullivantii* 'Goldsturm'

coneflower, perennial black-eyed susan

This North American native, selected and named in Germany, has deservedly become one of the most popular and reliable of perennials.

Among the rudbeckias, all native to North America, are some of the showiest perennials and annuals for

late summer colour. The perennial species grow from 30 cm (1 ft.) in height to over 2 m (6 ft.) and most are reliable and easily grown plants to brighten up the garden in late summer and autumn. *R. f.* var. *s.* 'Goldsturm' is a cumbersome name, and it seems ironic that such a popular North American native was selected in what was then Czechoslovakia and named in Germany for its compact free-flowering habit, eventually to return as a hero to its native land. Young nurseryman Heinz Hagemann took the plant to his famous employer Karl Foerster in Potsdam, Berlin, who gave it the name 'Goldsturm' ('Gold Storm') and introduced it around 1938. The original plant, it is said, was only about 45 cm (1½ ft.) high, but since it is often grown from seed, it has varied and can in moist soils reach 75–90 cm (2½–3 ft.). It makes leafy clumps of lance-shaped, dark glossy green leaves, above which a mass of deep-yellow-petalled flowers with central black cones make a striking contrast. *R. f.* var. *s.* 'Goldsturm' is the most compact of the species *R. fulgida* var. *sullivantii*, which has other subspecies, all native to eastern North America from New York south to Florida, and west to Ohio, Missouri and Texas, growing in open areas, moist meadows and valleys and on river banks.

R.f. var. *s.* 'Goldsturm' is an adaptable plant, growing in most soils where not too dry and excellent in moister soils, preferring full sun. By mid autumn when flowering has finished, black seedheads remain for the birds and are attractive in frost. Seeding can occur but is seldom a problem; if so, cut when flowering has finished. The spreading mats of roots and foliage may need curbing and occasional dieback of congested woody roots on older plants may ask for some replanting every few years, this best done in spring just as new growth appears. 60–75 cm (2–2½ ft.) × 45–60 cm (1½–2 ft.), spreading
F late summer, early autumn
Z 3–9

Further Recommendations
Other variations are equally valuable. *R. f.* Viette's Little Suzy 'Blovi' is a true dwarf, found as a seedling on Viette's nursery in Virginia, small in leaf and flower and only 30 cm (1 ft.) high, with yellow petals and a black cone. *R. f.* var. *deamii* has hairy, lighter green leaves. Flowering well into

autumn, it is taller at 90–120 cm (3–4 ft.), and vigorous.

So useful is its long-lasting display and general ease of culture that I'm happy to recommend *R. laciniata* 'Goldquelle' as an easy but underused late-flowering perennial with fully double golden-yellow flowers among bright green divided foliage, 120 cm (4 ft.) × 60 cm (2 ft.) high. Much taller and inclined to flop, so sometimes in need of staking, is the wonderful late-summer- and autumn-flowering

R. l. 'Herbstsonne' ('Autumn Sun'), with its warm yellow pendulous petals and chocolate-brown cigar stub cone. It provides autumn cheer with *Eupatorium maculatum* 'Gateway', and flowers until frosts. If too tall, cut back in late May or early June by half to reduce eventual height, although the sight of flowers against a blue autumn sky is one of this plant's delights. 180–240 cm (6–8 ft.) × 90–120 cm (3–4 ft.), **F** late summer to late autumn. **Z** 3–9.

←

Long a standard perennial sage, *Salvia* ×*sylvestris* 'Mainacht' is generally the earliest to bloom, with deep violet-blue flowers opening from base to tip—an excellent partner for *Achillea* 'Moonshine'.

Salvia ×*sylvestris* 'Mainacht'

sage

This is a reliable perennial with spikes of purple bracts opening to rich violet-blue flowers in spring, lasting for weeks.

Confusingly, the hardy perennial sages are variously listed under *Salvia nemorosa*, *Salvia* ×*superba*, *Salvia* ×*sylvestris* and *Salvia pratensis*. All are European natives and have freely interbred, so are mostly represented by an increasing number of cultivars.

The showy German-raised *S.* ×*sylvestris* 'Mainacht' ('May Night') is the earliest hardy salvia to flower. Considered to be a hybrid between *S. nemorosa* and *S. pratensis*, it has been in cultivation for at least 30 years and has become a standard. It forms a clump of dark green aromatic lance-shaped leaves, and mostly branched spikes whose emerging rich violet-blue flowers open from purple bracts. Flowers open from the base to tip over many weeks as stems continue to grow. Although time-consuming, early deadheading of spent stems and branches will prolong flowering.

Bressingham-raised *Achillea* 'Moonshine' and *Achillea* ANTHEA 'Anblo' are good early summer partners for *S.* ×*s.* 'Mainacht'. Like other *Salvia* hybrids, *S.* ×*s.* 'Mainacht' is generally tough and long-lived, preferring sun and good drainage, but tolerant, and in fact in the wild often growing in light woodland shade. Older plants can be divided every few years if required; as with replanting, this is best done in spring.
45–60 cm (1½–2 ft.) × 30–45 cm (1–1½ ft.)
F spring to summer
Z 5–9

Further Recommendations

Many other cultivars are worth recommending. Ernst Pagels, more famous perhaps for his breeding work on *Miscanthus*, was responsible for selecting and introducing some of the most popular cultivars including the compact, bushy pale blue *S.* ×*s.* 'Blauhügel' ('Blue Mound') and the free-flowering *S.* ×*s.* 'Ostfriesland', 45 cm (1½ ft.) high, an excellent grower with purple stems and bracts and violet flowers. A colour contrast is provided by *S.* ×*s.* 'Schneehügel' ('White Mound'), with soft white flowers and pale green bracts. All 45 cm (1½ ft.) × 45 cm (1½ ft.), **F** summer.

Those with more *S. pratensis* blood in them tend to be taller and more lax in habit, while *S. nemorosa* brings greater compactness. The choice of cultivars widens almost every year, but look out for newer selections like the already-popular *S.* ×*s.* 'Caradonna', 60 cm (2 ft.), with dark stems and eye-catching violet-blue flowers, and *S.* ×*s.* 'Pink Friesland', 45 cm (1½ ft.), glowing purple-pink.

Sedum 'Herbstfreude'

stonecrop

Sedum 'Herbstfreude', or 'Autumn Joy' in English, is an indispensable perennial for any garden, tough, hardy and succulent-looking with a season of interest lasting for more than six months from early summer until well into winter.

Raised over 50 years ago by famed German breeder and nurseryman Georg Arends, *S.* 'Herbstfreude' is a hybrid between two somewhat similar species, *S. spectabile* and *S. telephium*. *Sedum telephium* is found from western Europe east across Siberia to China and Japan, growing in open areas, grasslands and scrub, while

←

The deep pink flat-headed flowers of *Sedum* 'Herbstfreude' are much enjoyed by bees and butterflies. *Stipa tenuissima* is behind at Foggy Bottom.

S. spectabile is native to northern China and Korea. Both are clump-forming species with succulent grey-green leaves and erect stems 45–60 cm (1½–2 ft.) tall (and sometimes taller), flowering in late summer and autumn.

S. 'Herbstfreude' is a vigorous form, its grey-green leaves a contrast to other perennials or grasses before green-budded flat-topped flowerheads appear in late summer opening to glowing pink, deepening to red, and fading to crimson then dark brown in winter. Each head is made up of dozens of small flowers which in the full flowering stage of this type of *Sedum* are attractive to both bees and butterflies. *Sedum* 'Herbstfreude' and other similar forms do well in any type of good garden soil, preferring sun and good drainage, and in time will form large clumps. On older congested plants stems can elongate, forced out from the centre, and flop over, which can also occur if plants are over-fed and watered. These sedums are drought tolerant and generally trouble free, but older plants can be lifted and divided in early spring every few years if they become large and woody. The flat tops of spent flowers look great in winter, particularly when frosted or

with dollops of snow on top, so stems and flowerheads shouldn't be cut back until early spring, just as the new season's shoots are appearing. 45–60 cm (1½–2 ft.) × 45–60 cm (1½–2 ft.)
F late summer and autumn
Z 3–9

Further Recommendations

Among the sedums are some of the most showy and reliable late-summer-flowering perennials, their early foliage and dead winter seedheads extending their season of interest. Generally the *S. spectabile* hybrids are less vigorous than *S.* 'Herbstfreude' and somewhat shorter. *S. s.* 'Brilliant' has slightly curved heads of bright carmine pink to 45 cm (1½ ft.), and shorter at 30 cm (1 ft.) with white flowers and pale green foliage is *S. s.* 'Iceberg'. Now widely accepted as an outstanding cultivar and a favourite of mine is *S.* 'Matrona', raised in Germany and considered a hybrid of the purple-leaved *S. telephium* subsp. *maximum* 'Atropurpureum' and *S. spectabile*. An easily grown plant with large grey-green purple-flushed leaves and flat heads, its white buds open to soft pink, turning red-brown in

autumn, with tall, stiff purple stems reaching 75 cm (2½ ft.).
Lastly I've been impressed with another *S. spectabile* × *S. telephium* hybrid named *S.* 'Carl', well foliaged with grey-green leaves, upright sturdy stems to 45 cm (1½ ft.) and branched rounded heads of glowing rich pink flowers. All of these flower late summer to early autumn (**Z** 4–9).

Stachys byzantina 'Big Ears'

lamb's ears

A sterling foliage plant with large silver-grey felted leaves for a hot sunny spot, *S. b.* 'Big Ears' makes good ground cover and provides striking contrast to other plants.

As its name suggests, *Stachys byzantina* (syn. *S. lanata* and *S. olympica*) is native to Turkey (Byzantium being the old name for Istanbul), the south Caucasus and northern Iran where it grows in sunny, baked hillsides and scrub. It is notable for soft hairy, felted leaves and for spikes carrying heads of small pink or purple flowers on stems of 45–90 cm (1½–3 ft.).

The name of *S. b.* 'Big Ears' (sometimes known as *S. b.* 'Helena von

Stein') aptly describes the large oval woolly grey leaves which can be as much as 20–25 cm (8–10 in.) long. For a vigorous large-leaved plant it is hardly surprising that flower spikes with magenta flowers in summer reach 90 cm (3 ft.) or taller, but the relatively few stems can be cut away as required. These are plants for heat, sun and good drainage, excelling in poor soil, but in hot humid climates most are subject to mildew, although *S. b.* 'Big Ears' is considered the most heat-tolerant and mildew-resistant cultivar to date.

Dead or rotting leaves should be removed from *Stachys byzantina* cultivars as soon as they appear. Ensure good drainage year-round. If plants become old or woody, dig them up in spring, discard old material and replant younger divisions. Vigorous plants may need curbing annually with a spade. *S. b.* 'Big Ears' is a high-impact plant that needs a bold companion such as *Geranium* 'Rozanne', or a purple-foliaged *Berberis*, *Cotinus* or *Physocarpus*.

90 cm (3 ft.) × 60–75 cm (2–2.5 ft.)
F early summer
Z 4–8

Further Recommendations

For gardeners who feel that the flowers detract from the foliage, the generally non-flowering *S. b.* 'Silver Carpet' will be desirable, and well named, the spreading foliage forming mats of bright silver-grey to only 15 cm (6 in.) tall. *S. b.* 'Primrose Heron' was named by Englishwoman Sue Gemmell after her mother; in sun, the early spring leaves are a glowing yellow, paler in light shade, gradually fading over a few weeks to silver-grey, with pink flowers on 45-cm (1½-ft.) stems.

← At the Chanticleer Garden in Pennsylvania, *Stachys byzantina* 'Big Ears' makes an effective silver-grey carpet in midsummer punctuated by *Yucca flaccida* 'Golden Sword' and contrasting purple-leaved *Berberis thunbergii* 'Rose Glow'.

→

The ripening inflorescences of *Stipa tenuissima* move and wave like a river in windy conditions, adding light and movement to more static evergreens on a late summer day in Foggy Bottom.

Stipa tenuissima

Mexican feather grass

Although short-lived, *S. tenuissima* can add grace, movement and beauty to gardens large and small as it changes with the seasons.

The relatively short two- to three-year lifespan of this ornamental grass is compensated for by its freedom to seed, as younger seedlings are always available for replacement. The species originates from New Mexico, Texas and Mexico, and strangely also from Argentina, growing in open dry areas and on rocky hillsides. Erect new growth of slender needle-like rich green stems is soon followed by light green inflorescences maturing to gold in summer, then remaining an attractive silvery grey into winter. Although drought-tolerant, plants can go dormant early in hotter regions. Once in flower, the feathery plumes begin to sway with every breeze and a drift backlit by the sun can be extraordinarily spectacular, as can the frost on winter foliage.

S. tenuissima (syn. *Nassella tenuissima*) prefers sun and good drainage but is remarkably versatile, with self sown seedlings (which can easily be

removed if not required) often found growing in the most unpromising situations on both light and heavy soils. Cut back old growth on established plants by half in early spring. Young open-ground seedlings can be moved and replanted when spring growth is greening up, and divisions of larger plants can be made, but not too small, ensuring plants go in at the same depth. Older plants may gradually die; best then to remove and replace in spring. There are many uses for this intriguing feather grass: to add movement to conifers and shrubs, as a mini grassland through which spiky plants such as kniphofias or acanthus can grow, or in a container, freely flowing over the edge.

60 cm (2 ft.) × 45–60 cm (1½–2 ft.)
F summer into autumn
Z 6–9

Further Recommendations

At its best, *Stipa gigantea*, the giant feather grass, is a glorious ornamental species, its rather less-than-striking clump-forming green spear-shaped floppy leaves to 75–90 cm (2½–3 ft.) forming a vital base for the towering panicles to follow. In early summer these are borne on long slender stems, 180–240 cm (6–8 ft.) or taller, the green oat-like heads enlarging and turning to gold, blowing gracefully in the wind and sparse enough to be able to see through, holding up well into winter. Native to southern Spain, Portugal and North Africa in mountainous regions, *S. gigantea* needs a warm, well-drained reasonably sheltered position in cooler climates. Clean old stems and foliage in spring. Flowers summer into autumn. **Z** 6–9.

Tiarella cordifolia

foam flower

T. cordifolia is a favourite shade or woodland plant with fine ground-covering foliage and a magnificent show of white flowers in spring.

Native to eastern North America, it grows in rich moist soils in woodland and mountainous regions from Nova Scotia in Canada, east to Ontario and south to Georgia. Once established it spreads by surface running shoots, rooting as it goes. The light green leaves are similar to those of *Heuchera*, and form a carpet above which erect spikes, 15–30 cm (6–12 in.) high, are massed with pretty white flowers in spring and early summer, the mature leaves becoming marked with red in autumn and winter. In the garden *T. cordifolia* is extremely useful as evergreen ground cover, in light shade beneath trees or shrubs where not too dry, although once established it is reasonably drought tolerant. In early autumn or early spring, rooted runners can be detached to plant else-

Delicate oat-like inflorescences of *Stipa gigantea* rise above dark green basal foliage, allowing us to glimpse the yellow-flowered *Phlomis russelliana* and other perennials in this association in landscape designer Tom Stuart-Smith's garden in England.

→

Tiarella cordifolia, seen beneath a viburnum in spring in the Summer Garden at Bressingham, displays a mass of dainty white flowers.

where, or curbed if it is spreading into unwanted places.

10–15 cm (4–6 in.) × 60 cm (2 ft.), spreading

F spring to early summer

Z 4–8

Further Recommendations

If the genes of *T. cordifolia* represent the spreading habit of newer hybrids, *T. wherryi* (syn. *T. cordifolia* subsp. *collina*) represents the clump-forming types. The latter is a southeastern North American native, mainly from the states of Tennessee, North Carolina and Alabama, growing in rocky woodland and shady valleys, more tolerant of sun and heat than *T. cordifolia*. It has showier flowers, and bronze and purple markings on older evergreen leaves.

Although other species have been involved, *T. cordifolia* and *T. wherryi* have formed the basis of the new cultivars now available, many of which are worthy of a place in gardens for shade where the soil is not too dry in hotter climates, or sun or shade in cooler temperate zones. Which hybrids to choose?

T. 'Oakleaf', a form of *T. wherryi*, has shining dark green deeply lobed leaves turning bronze-red in winter, flowers on 30-cm (1-ft.) spikes, light pink fading to whte, while *T.* 'Elizabeth Oliver', raised like so many by the team of Charles and Martha Oliver from Pennsylvania, has frilly-edged light green maple-like leaves centrally marked with maroon, with pale pink fragrant flowers on 30–45-cm (1–1½-ft.) stems, slowly spreading by runners. Another Oliver introduction is the clump-forming *T.* 'Pink Brushes', making neat

mounds of deeply dissected maroon-centred leaves, and in spring a massed display of pink-budded flowers opening to white bottlebrush heads to 40 cm (16 in.). For more heavily marked foliage, try the large-leaved vigorous T. 'Neon Lights', lighter-green-edged leaves and pink buds opening to white flowers, maroon-centred, and the running, ground-covering T. 'Jeepers Creepers', to 20 cm (8 in.) high, with dissected leaves and bright maroon-red centres, and 30-cm (1-ft.) flower spikes in spring.

Verbena bonariensis

vervain

A short-lived perennial that freely regenerates from seed when given the chance, the tall erect stems topped with small purple flowers provide a display from midsummer until frosts.

Few *Verbena* species are truly hardy and *V. bonariensis*, from Argentina, is only hardy to USDA hardiness zone 7—but since it seeds so freely, it still seems legitimate to grow as a perennial, since seedlings will flower late in their first year. It forms rosettes of

hairy leaves and erect, rough, hairy stems, varying in height from 90 to 180 cm (3–6 ft.) or taller, each stem topped by small heads of purple funnel-shaped flowers, attractive to butterflies, in late midsummer until autumn frosts. Even into winter the brown to black seedheads remain attractive.

V. bonariensis mixes well with grasses, lower-growing perennials, and shrubs where its purple flowers contrast with golden or purple foliage. Growing easily in almost any soil that is not too dry, it is a classic see-through

←

No garden should be without the see-through *Verbena bonariensis*, even though it is not long lived. The flowers here in late summer will continue until frosts and will then become attractive seedheads.

→

Without earlier trimming, *Veronicastrum virginicum* 'Lavendelturm' reaches an imposing stature, even towering above *Crocosmia* 'Lucifer' in midsummer in the Dell Garden at Bressingham.

plant, the tall well-spaced stems allowing the viewer to glimpse other plants and views that lie behind it. In milder regions, the species may live two or three years, but in most cases the annual seedlings will be more vigorous and catch up. Don't cut back stems until midwinter, by which time seed will have dropped to come up the following spring in the surrounding area. Unwanted seedlings can be taken out, given away or replanted elsewhere. 90–180 cm (3–6 ft.) × 30 cm (1 ft.) **F** late midsummer until winter **Z** 7–10

Veronicastrum virginicum 'Lavendelturm'

culver's root

Tall, elegant branched spikes and subdued lavender flowers make *V. v.* 'Lavendelturm' an excellent perennial to contrast with *Crocosmia* 'Lucifer' and summer yellow-golds of *Heliopsis* and *Helenium*.

Similarity in name to the closely related yet more popular *Veronica* has until recently obscured the excellence of the *Veronicastrum virginicum* cultivars. Long-lived, they give elegance and colour to the garden.

V. v. 'Lavendelturm' ('Lavender Towers') is but one, and German plantsman and nurseryman Ernst Pagels's eye for a good plant is evident in this selection.

The species is a North American native, widespread across eastern and midwestern North America where it grows in meadows and open woods. *V. v.* 'Lavendelturm' has spire-like growth, with whorls of lance-shaped leaves terminating in branched spikes to 180 cm (6 ft.), the lavender-purple flowers opening from the base of the narrow head upwards from midsummer to early autumn, and longer if spent flower spikes are deadheaded. The species and cultivars are clump-forming perennials, and as the spikes are not overcrowded they have an airy feel, hence their elegance, although those wishing for a shorter plant can prune back growth in early summer. Best in sun, they seldom need staking, although planting in some shade may stretch stems and create a tendency to flop. Generally easily grown, they prefer some moisture at their roots. Divide in spring.
150–180 cm (5–6 ft.) × 45–60 cm (1½–2 ft.)

F midsummer to early autumn
Z 5–8

Further Recommendations

Other cultivars worth considering are *V. v.* 'Apollo', 120–150 cm (4–5 ft.) tall, with dark green leaves and soft lilac-pink flowers; *V. v.* 'Fascination', 120–180 cm (4–6 ft.), with unusual lilac-blue two-toned spikes and reddish green leaves; and the shorter 90–120-cm (3–4-ft.) *V. v.* 'Spring Dew', with deep green leaves and white flowers.

Vinca minor 'La Grave'

periwinkle

The best of the small-leaved periwinkles, *V. m.* 'La Grave' is valuable for its abundant display of deep blue spring flowers and reasonably restrained ground-covering ability, its evergreen leaves bright and glossy.

We all have a place for ground-covering plants, and vincas can be useful—although some are too vigorous and relatively sparse in their ability to smother seedling weeds. *Vinca minor* is a woodland, shade-loving plant from central and eastern Europe to central Asia, spreading by runners, with small five-petalled flowers occurring among the mats of foliage in mid spring. Several cultivars with double or single flowers of white, blue, red and purple, as well as some with variegated leaves, are available—but for me, far and away the best and most floriferous performer is *V. m.* 'La Grave' (syn. *V. m.* 'Bowles's Variety'), with purple-blue spring flowers that are larger than most, and its shiny evergreen leaves that make excellent ground cover for the rest of the year. Some shade is preferred where not too dry and once established it will spread to cover drier areas too.

The flowers are perfectly timed to arrive at the same time as *Primula vulgaris*. Curb as necessary, ideally before running shoots begin to root into the ground. Rooted runners or lifting clumps for division can be methods of propagation, best carried out in late summer or early spring.
15 cm (6 in.) × 60 cm (2 ft.), spreading
F spring
Z 5–8

↑
Vinca minor 'La Grave', the most compact and free-flowering periwinkle, fights for territory with yellow-flowered *Primula vulgaris*, momentarily making a great partnership.

THE LAST BUT
NOT LEAST PAGES

← Going out with a bang: the glowing orange-red and yellow poker heads of *Kniphofia rooperi* show up in late autumn against North American asters in the Dell Garden at Bressingham.

Perennials and Grasses for Special Purposes

USDA Hardiness Zones and Equivalent UK Conditions

Suppliers of Perennials and Grasses

Index of Plant Names

Acknowledgements

Echinacea purpurea 'White Swan'

Eryngium 'Jos Eijking'

Perennials and Grasses for Special Purposes

The following lists will give some guidance at a glance if you are looking for particular plant attributes for garden planning, design and planting. They are only a guide; so variable can conditions be in different countries and regions that no guarantees can be made.

Drought-Resistant

Drought in Britain or northern Europe is unlikely to be as extreme as in the southern United States, where summer temperatures are higher by day and night, and generally for longer periods. In all regions, plantings must be given adequate watering until fully established.

Acanthus spinosus and other *Acanthus* species and cultivars

Achillea 'Moonshine' and other *Achillea* species and cultivars

Amsonia hubrichtii

Anaphalis margaritacea

Artemisia ludoviciana 'Valerie Finnis' and 'Silver Queen'

Aster ericoides and cultivars

Aster lateriflorus 'Prince'

Baptisia australis and other *Baptisia* species and cultivars

Bergenia 'Bressingham Ruby' and most other *Bergenia* cultivars

Brunnera macrophylla 'Jack Frost' and other *B. m.* cultivars

Coreopsis verticillata 'Zagreb' and other *C. v.* cultivars

Cortaderia selloana 'Pumila'

Cynara cardunculus

Echinacea purpurea 'Kim's Knee High' and other *E. p.* hybrids and cultivars

Echinops ritro and other *Echinops* species and cultivars

Epimedium ×*perralchicum* 'Fröhnleiten' and other *Epimedium* species and cultivars

Eryngium bourgatii and cultivars

Eryngium ×*zabelii* 'Jos Eijking'

Euphorbia polychroma and cultivars

Gaura lindheimeri and cultivars

Geranium macrorrhizum 'Bevan's Variety' and other *G. m.* hybrids and cultivars

Geranium 'Rozanne' and 'Ann Folkard'

Geranium sanguineum and cultivars

Helianthus 'Lemon Queen'

Heliopsis helianthoides var. *scabra* 'Spitzentänzerin' and other *H. h.* var. *s.* cultivars

Helleborus ×*hybridus*

Hemerocallis 'Hyperion' and most other *H.* cultivars

Nepeta ×*faasenii* and cultivars

Nepeta ×*racemosa* 'Walker's Low' and other *N.* ×*r.* cultivars

Panicum virgatum 'Northwind' and other *P. v.* cultivars

Pennisetum alopecuroides and cultivars

Pennisetum orientale

Primula vulgaris

Sedum 'Herbstfreude' and most other *Sedum* species and cultivars

Stachys byzantina 'Big Ears' and other *S. b.* cultivars

Stipa tenuissima

*Polygonatum
odoratum var.
pluriflorum
'Variegatum'*

Pulmonaria 'Blue
Ensign'

Shade-Tolerant

In the kind of climates found in Nova Scotia, Norway or Scotland few plants demand shade, while in Australia and much of the mid and southern United States they will. Once again this list is only guide and local advice should be sought for confirmation. (An asterisk* indicates that a plant is likely to tolerate dry shade.)

Actaea simplex 'Brunette' and other *A. s.* cultivars

Alchemilla mollis

Amsonia orientalis

Amsonia tabernaemontana

*Asarum europaeum**

*Aster ×herveyi**

Astilbe chinensis var. *taquetii* 'Superba' and other
    A. c. var. *t.* cultivars

Astrantia major 'Ruby Wedding' and other
    A. m. cultivars

Bergenia 'Bressingham White', 'Morgenrote' and
    'Silberlicht'

Brunnera macrophylla 'Jack Frost' and other
    B. m. cultivars

Campanula poscharskyana 'Blue Waterfall'

Deschampsia cespitosa 'Goldtau' and other
    D. c. cultivars

Dicentra 'Luxuriant' and other *Dicentra* cultivars

Epimedium ×perralchicum 'Fröhnleiten' and other
    Epimedium species and cultivars*

Geranium maccrorrhizum 'Bevan's Variety' and other
    G. m. hybrids and cultivars*

Geranium maculatum and cultivars

Geranium sylvaticum 'Mayflower' and *G. s.* cultivars

Gillenia trifoliata

Hakonechloa macra 'Alboaurea', *H. macra* and other
    cultivars

Helleborus ×hybridus

Heuchera americana 'Dale's Strain'

Hosta 'Halcyon' and most *Hosta* species and cultivars

Ligularia 'The Rocket'

Liriope muscari and cultivars

Luzula sylvatica 'Aurea' and other *L. s.* cultivars*

Ophiopogon planiscapus 'Nigrescens'

Polygonatum ×hybridum 'Striatum'*

Polygonatum odoratum var. *pluriflorum* 'Variegatum'*

Primula vulgaris

Pulmonaria 'Diana Clare' and other *Pulmonaria* species
    and cultivars

Solidago rugosa 'Fireworks'

Tiarella cordifolia and other *Tiarella* species, hybrids and
    cultivars*

Veronicastrum virginicum 'Lavendelturm' and other
    V. v. cultivars

Vinca minor 'La Grave' and other *Vinca* species and
    cultivars*

Astilbe chinensis var. *taquetii* 'Superba'

Euphorbia griffithii 'Fireglow'

Moisture-Tolerant

Moist conditions can be described as damp, wet or boggy, or even as 'well-drained soil that does not dry out'. Many of the plants in this list are adaptable to general garden conditions too. Few are for year-round wet, waterside conditions.

Aconitum carmichaelii 'Arendsii' and other *Aconitum* species and cultivars

Acorus gramineus 'Oborozuki' and 'Ogon'

Actaea simplex 'Brunette' and most other *Actaea* species and cultivars

Astilbe chinensis var. *taquetii* 'Superba' and other *Astilbe* species and cultivars

Astrantia major 'Ruby Wedding' and other *A. m.* cultivars

Carex elata 'Aurea'

Deschampsia cespitosa 'Goldtau' and other *D. c.* cultivars

Eupatorium purpureum subsp. *maculatum* 'Gateway' and other *E. p.* subsp. *m.* cultivars

Euphorbia griffithii 'Dixter' and 'Fireglow'

Geranium sylvaticum and cultivars

Gillenia trifoliata

Hemerocallis 'Hyperion' and most other *Hemerocallis* cultivars

Hosta 'Halcyon' and most other *Hosta* species and cultivars

Iris sibirica 'Silver Edge' and other *I. s.* cultivars

Ligularia 'Britt Marie Crawford' and other *Ligularia* species and cultivars

Miscanthus sinensis 'Morning Light' and other *M. s.* cultivars

Molinia caerulea 'Variegata' and other *M. c.* cultivars

Monarda didyma 'Gardenview Scarlet' and other *M. d.* cultivars

Persicaria amplexicaulis 'Taurus' and other *P. a.* cultivars

Phlox paniculata 'Franz Schubert' and other *P. p.* cultivars

Rodgersia podophylla and other *Rodgersia* species

Rudbeckia fulgida var. *sullivantii* 'Goldsturm' and other *R. f.* varieties and cultivars

Eupatorium rugosum
'Chocolate'

Imperata cylindrica
'Rubra'

Variegated or Coloured Foliage

Foliage plays a vital role in joining and extending the flowering season and is helpful in leavening bold flower colours, although some foliage can shout loudly too.

Acanthus mollis 'Hollard's Gold'
Acorus gramineus 'Oborozuki' and 'Ogon'
Aster laterifolius 'Prince'
Astilbe simplicifolia 'Sprite'
Astrantia major 'Sunningdale Variegated'
Bergenia 'Bressingham Ruby' (in winter)
Brunnera macrophylla 'Hadspen Cream'
Brunnera macrophylla 'Jack Frost'
Calamagrostis ×*acutiflora* 'Overdam'
Eupatorium rugosum 'Chocolate'
Euphorbia polychroma 'Bonfire'
Festuca glauca 'Elijah Blue', 'Blauglut' and 'Blaufuchs'
Geranium 'Blue Sunrise' and 'Ann Folkard'
Hakonechloa macra 'Alboaurea', 'Allgold' and 'Albovariegata'
Heliopsis helianthoides Loraine Sunshine 'Helhan'
Heuchera 'Chocolate Ruffles' and other selected cultivars
Hosta 'Halcyon' and other cultivars,
Imperata cylindrica 'Rubra'
Ligularia 'Britt Marie Crawford'
Liriope muscari 'Variegata'
Luzula sylvatica 'Aurea', 'Marginata' and 'Taggart's Cream'
Miscanthus sinensis 'Morning Light', 'Strictus', 'Gold Bar', 'Variegatus' and 'Dixieland'
Ophiopogon planiscapus 'Nigrescens'
Phlox paniculata 'Nora Leigh'

Polygonatum ×*hybridum* 'Striatum'
Polygonatum odoratum var. *pluriflorum* 'Variegatum'
Pulmonaria 'Bertram Anderson', 'Diana Clare', 'Lewis Palmer', *longifolia*, 'Opal', 'Roy Davidson' and *saccharata* 'Leopard'
Stachys byzantina 'Big Ears' and other *S. b.* cultivars

Aster novae-angliae 'Andenken an Alma Potschke'

Kniphofia 'Brimstone'

Attractive to Bees and Butterflies

We usually welcome bees, butterflies and birds to our gardens. Perennials in particular offer them important food, adding value to the environment. In books and catalogues, describing a plant as "attractive to bees and butterflies" sounds rather better than "attractive to flies and wasps", which of course some of the following also are.

Best for Bees

Achillea	*Heliopsis*
Aster	*Hemerocallis*
Bergenia	*Heuchera*
Campanula	*Kniphofia*
Coreopsis	*Ligularia*
Crocosmia	*Monarda*
Echinacea	*Nepeta*
Echinops	*Phlox paniculata*
Eryngium	*Pulmonaria*
Geranium (some)	*Rudbeckia*
Helenium	*Salvia*
Helianthus	*Sedum*

Best for Butterflies

Achillea	*Helenium*
Aster	*Kniphofia*
Coreopsis	*Nepeta*
Echinacea	*Phlox paniculata*
Echinops	*Sedum*
Eryngium	

Cynara cardunculus

Miscanthus sinensis
'Malepartus'

Attractive Seedheads

Late summer and autumn may be the nadir of many perennials and grasses, but a different level of interest and attraction is provided by fascinating and attractive seedheads, many of which offer food for birds into winter. If they look good, do not rush to cut them down—unless the seeds become a nuisance when they drop and freely germinate.

Achillea, most species and cultivars

Actaea matsumurae 'Elstead' and 'White Pearl'

Actaea simplex 'Brunette', 'Hillside Black Beauty' and 'James Compton'

Agapanthus 'Bressingham Blue', *inapertus* and 'Loch Hope'

Artemisia ludoviciana 'Silver Queen' and 'Valerie Finnis'

Artemisia triplinervis 'Sommerschnee'

Astilbe species and cultivars

Astrantia major and cultivars

Baptisia species and cultivars

Calamagrostis ×*acutifolia* 'Overdam' and 'Karl Foerster'

Coreopsis verticillata and cultivars

Cortaderia selloana 'Pumila'

Crocosmia 'Lucifer' and 'Firebird'

Cynara cardunculus

Deschampsia cespitosa 'Goldtau' and other cultivars

Echinacea purpurea and cultivars

Echinops ritro and *E. r.* 'Veitch's Blue'

Eryngium ×*zabelii* 'Jos Eijking'

Eupatorium maculatum 'Gateway' and cultivars

Helenium 'Moerheim Beauty' and other *Helenium* cultivars

Iris sibirica and cultivars

Kniphofia caulescens

Liatris spicata 'Kobold'

Ligularia 'Britt Marie Crawford' and other *Ligularia* species and cultivars

Liriope muscari

Miscanthus sinensis and most *Miscanthus* cultivars

Molinia caerulea 'Variegata' and other *M. c.* cultivars

Monarda didyma 'Gardenview Scarlet' and other *M. d.* cultivars

Ophiopogon planiscapus 'Nigrescens'

Panicum virgatum 'Northwind' and other *P. v.* cultivars

Pennisetum alopecuroides 'Hameln', 'Little Bunny' and 'Moudry'

Pennisetum orientale and *P. o.* 'Karley Rose'

Rodgersia pinnata 'Superba' and other *R. p.* cultivars

Rudbeckia fulgida var. *sullivantii* 'Goldsturm' and other *R. f.* varieties and cultivars

Rudbeckia laciniata 'Herbstsonne'

Sedum 'Herbstfreude' and other *Sedum* cultivars

Stipa gigantea

Stipa tenuissima

Verbena bonariensis

Veronicastrum virginicum 'Lavendelturm'

Helleborus xhybridus

Hosta sieboldiana 'Elegans'

Useful for Ground Cover

Plants that spread to create a dense mat as well as those that cover the ground for much of the year are included in this list. Some are for sun, while others prefer shade. Always ensure that the planting ground is clear of all weeds (especially perennial ones) before planting, and keep weeding as necessary until ground cover is established. (An asterisk* indicates evergreen foliage, while two stars** indicate that it is semi-evergreen according to region and situation.)

Acorus gramineus 'Oborozuki' and 'Ogon'*

Alchemilla mollis

Anaphalis triplinervis

*Asarum europaeum**

Astilbe chinensis 'Pumila'

Bergenia 'Bressingham Ruby' and most other bergenias*

Brunnera macrophylla 'Jack Frost' and other cultivars

Campanula poscharskyana 'Blue Waterfall'**

Carex comans 'Bronze Form' and other cultivars*

Carex oshimensis 'Evergold'*

Coreopsis verticillata 'Zagreb' and other cultivars

Deschampsia cespitosa 'Goldtau'**

Epimedium xperralchicum 'Fröhnleiten' and most other epimediums*

Festuca glauca 'Elijah Blue' and other cultivars*

Geranium macrorrhizum 'Bevan's Variety'*

Geranium 'Rozanne' and many other hardy geraniums

Hakonechloa macra 'Alboaurea', *H. macra* and other cultivars

*Helleborus xhybridus**

Heuchera 'Chocolate Ruffles' and more vigorous cultivars**

Hosta 'Halcyon' and most larger-leaved cultivars

Leucanthemum xsuperbum 'Snowcap'

*Liriope muscari**

Luzula sylvatica 'Aurea' and other *L. s.* cultivars*

Nepeta racemosa 'Walker's Low'

Ophiopogon planiscapus 'Nigrescens'**

Pennisetum alopecuroides 'Hameln' and other *P. a.* cultivars

Pennisetum orientale

Persicaria amplexicaulis 'Taurus' and other cultivars

Persicaria bistorta 'Superbum'

Polygonatum xhybridum 'Striatum'

Polygonatum odoratum var. *pluriflorum* 'Variegatum'

Pulmonaria 'Diana Clare' and most other vigorous pulmonarias**

Rudbeckia fulgida var. *deamii*

Rudbeckia fulgida var. *sullivantii* 'Goldsturm'

Salvia xsylvestris 'Blauhügel', *S. xs.* 'Schneehügel' and other cultivars

Sedum 'Herbstfreude' and some other large-leaved sedums

Stachys byzantina 'Big Ears' and 'Silver Carpet'**

Tiarella cordifolia and other tiarellas*

Vinca minor 'La Grave' and other vincas*

*Epimedium
×perralchicum
'Fröhnleiten'*

*Echinacea purpurea
'Kim's Knee High'*

For Small Gardens

If you have a small garden, it does not necessarily follow that none of your plants should grow taller than 60 cm (2 ft.); there may be room for a small tree, conifer, shrub or climber, or even some taller perennials or grasses. However, below is a list of perennials and grasses that normally will not exceed this height. (Bear in mind, though, that with feed, water and shade some plants may grow taller than expected.)

	Approximate maximum height
Achillea ANTHEA 'Anblo'	60 cm (2 ft.)
Acorus gramineus 'Oborozuki' and 'Ogon'	30 cm (1 ft.)
Agapanthus 'Isis'	60 cm (2 ft.)
Agapanthus 'Lilliput'	45 cm (1½ ft.)
Alchemilla mollis	60 cm (2 ft.)
Amsonia orientalis	60 cm (2 ft.)
Anaphalis triplinervis 'Sommerschnee'	30 cm (1 ft.)
Asarum europaeum	20 cm (8 in.)
Aster amellus 'Veilchenkönigin'	45 cm (1½ ft.)
Aster ×frikartii 'Flora's Delight'	45 cm (1½ ft.)
Aster laterifolius 'Prince'	45 cm (1½ ft.)
Aster simplicifolia 'Sprite'	30 cm (1 ft.)
Astilbe chinensis 'Pumila'	45 cm (1½ ft.)
Astilbe chinensis 'Visions'	45 cm (1½ ft.)
Astrantia major 'Ruby Wedding'	60 cm (2 ft.)
Bergenia 'Bressingham Ruby' and other *Bergenia* cultivars	60 cm (2 ft.)
Brunnera macrophylla 'Hadspen Cream'	60 cm (2 ft.)
Brunnera macrophylla 'Jack Frost'	60 cm (2 ft.)
Campanula lactiflora 'Pouffe'	45 cm (1½ ft.)

	Approximate maximum height
Campanula poscharskyana 'Blue Waterfall'	30 cm (1 ft.)
Carex buchananii	60 cm (2 ft.)
Carex comans 'Bronze Form'	45 cm (1½ ft.)
Carex comans 'Frosted Curls'	45 cm (1½ ft.)
Carex flagillifera	45 cm (1½ ft.)
Carex oshimensis 'Evergold'	30 cm (1 ft.)
Carex tenuiculmis	45 cm (1½ ft.)
Coreopsis verticillata 'Golden Gain'	60 cm (2 ft.)
Coreopsis verticillata 'Grandiflora'	60 cm (2 ft.)
Coreopsis verticillata 'Moonbeam'	45 cm (1½ ft.)
Coreopsis verticillata 'Zagreb'	30 cm (1 ft.)
Crocosmia 'Spitfire'	60 cm (2 ft.)
Crocosmia 'Vulcan'	60 cm (2 ft.)
Deschampsia cespitosa 'Goldtau'	60 cm (2 ft.)
Dicentra 'Luxuriant' and other cultivars	45 cm (1½ ft.)
Echinacea purpurea 'Kim's Knee High	60 cm (2 ft.)
Echinacea purpurea 'Kim's Mop Head'	60 cm (2 ft.)
Epimedium ×perralchicum 'Fröhnleiten' and other epimediums	45 cm (1½ ft.)
Eryngium bourgatii and cultivars	60 cm (2 ft.)
Euphorbia polychroma and cultivars	60 cm (2 ft.)
Festuca glauca 'Elijah Blue' and other *F. g.* cultivars	30 cm (1 ft.)
Gaura lindheimeri 'Siskiyou Pink'	60 cm (2 ft.)
Geranium 'Ann Folkard'	60 cm (2 ft.)
Geranium 'Blue Sunrise'	60 cm (2 ft.)
Geranium ×cantabrigiense 'Cambridge' and other *G. ×c.* cultivars	30 cm (1 ft.)

Hosta 'Shade Fanfare'

Heuchera 'Chocolate Ruffles'

Approximate maximum height	
Geranium macrorrhizum 'Bevan's Variety' and other *G. m.* cultivars	45 cm (1½ ft.)
Geranium maculatum	60 cm (2 ft.)
Geranium sanguineum 'Alan Bloom' and other *G. s.* cultivars	45 cm (1½ ft.)
Geranium sylvaticum 'Album'	60 cm (2 ft.)
Geranium sylvaticum 'Mayflower'	60 cm (2 ft.)
Hakonechloa macra 'Alboaurea' and other *H. m.* cultivars	45 cm (1½ ft.)
Helenium 'Pipsqueak'	60 cm (2 ft.)
Helleborus ×*hybridus*	45 cm (1½ ft.)
Hemerocallis 'Happy Returns'	60 cm (2 ft.)
Hemerocallis 'Pardon Me'	60 cm (2 ft.)
Hemerocallis 'Stella de Oro'	60 cm (2 ft.)
Heuchera 'Chocolate Ruffles' and most other *Heuchera* cultivars	60 cm (2 ft.)
Hosta 'Halcyon'	45 cm (1½ ft.)
Hosta 'Francee'	60 cm (2 ft.)
Hosta 'Golden Tiara'	45 cm (1½ ft.)
Hosta 'Patriot'	60 cm (2 ft.)
Hosta 'Shade Fanfare'	60 cm (2 ft.)
Imperata cylindrica 'Rubra'	45 cm (1½ ft.)
Iris sibirica 'Baby Sister'	45 cm (1½ ft.)
Kniphofia 'Bressingham Comet'	60 cm (2 ft.)
Kniphofia 'Little Maid'	60 cm (2 ft.)
Leucanthemum ×*superbum* 'Snow Lady'	45 cm (1½ ft.)
Leucanthemum ×*superbum* 'Snowcap'	45 cm (1½ ft.)

Approximate maximum height	
Liriope muscari and cultivars	45 cm (1½ ft.)
Luzula sylvatica 'Aurea'	45 cm (1½ ft.)
Luzula sylvatica 'Marginata'	45 cm (1½ ft.)
Luzula sylvatica 'Taggart's Cream'	45 cm (1½ ft.)
Luzula nivea	60 cm (2 ft.)
Molinia caerulea 'Variegata'	60 cm (2 ft.)
Ophiopogon planiscapus 'Nigrescens'	30 cm (1 ft.)
Pennisetum alopecuroides 'Little Bunny'	45 cm (1½ ft.)
Primula vulgaris	20 cm (8 in.)
Primula vulgaris subsp. *sibthorpii*	20 cm (8 in.)
Pulmonaria 'Diana Clare' and other pulmonarias	45 cm (1½ ft.)
Rudbeckia fulgida VIETTE'S LITTLE SUZY 'Blovi'	30 cm (12 in.)
Salvia ×*sylvestris* 'Mainacht' and other *S.* ×*s.* cultivars	60 cm (2 ft.)
Sedum 'Carl'	45 cm (1½ ft.)
Sedum 'Herbstfreude'	60 cm (2 ft.)
Sedum spectabile 'Brilliant'	45 cm (1½ ft.)
Sedum spectabile 'Iceberg'	45 cm (1½ ft.)
Stachys byzantina 'Big Ears' (foliage)	30 cm (1 ft.)
Stachys byzantina 'Primrose Heron' (foliage)	30 cm (1 ft.)
Stachys byzantina 'Silver Carpet' (foliage)	30 cm (1 ft.)
Stipa tenuissima	60 cm (2 ft.)
Tiarella cordifolia	30 cm (1 ft.)
Tiarella wherryi and cultivars	30 cm (1 ft.)
Vinca minor 'La Grave'	15 cm (6 in.)

Baptisia australis

Liatris spicata

Resistance to Deer and Rabbits

Some years ago, we seldom saw deer or rabbits in our garden at Foggy Bottom and considered the occasional Roe deer down in our woods to be a beautiful and even romantic sight. But times have changed and, judging from comments from gardeners in Britain, Europe and North America, their increasing numbers have seen deer become pests. The list below, compiled according to first-hand experience as well as reference, can only be used as a guide. It seems that deer are getting more adventurous, if not yet (thank goodness) gourmets of the total garden palette on offer. It is therefore asking for trouble to define those plants listed below as deer- or rabbit-"proof".

Deer-Resistant

Acanthus
Achillea
Aconitum
Actaea
Alchemilla mollis
Amsonia
Artemisia
Aster
Astilbe
Baptisia
Campanula
Carex
Coreopsis
Cortaderia
Crocosmia
Dicentra
Echinacea purpurea
Echinops
Epimedium
Eryngium
Eupatorium
Euphorbia
Geranium (most)
Helianthus
Helleborus ×hybridus
Kniphofia
Leucanthemum
Liatris
Liriope
Monarda didyma
Nepeta
Polygonatum
Primula vulgaris
Pulmonaria
Rodgersia
Rudbeckia
Salvia ×sylvestris
Stachys byzantina
Tiarella
Vinca

Rabbit-Resistant

Rabbits not only nibble but also dig at roots. Chicken wire around plants will prevent damage to treasures, but it is expensive, unsightly and almost impossible on a large scale.

Aconitum
Agapanthus
Alchemilla
Amsonia
Anaphalis
Astilbe
Bergenia
Brunnera
Cardunculus
Cortaderia
Crocosmia
Epimedium
Eupatorium
Euphorbia
Helenium
Helianthus
Helleborus ×hybridus
Hemerocallis
Hosta
Iris sibirica
Kniphofia
Luzula
Miscanthus
Nepeta
Persicaria
Pulmonaria
Sedum
Stachys byzantina
Vinca

Below you will find a listing of the main hardiness zones (left-hand column) that were developed by the United States Department of Agriculture (USDA), with an equivalent assessment for the United Kingdom. These zones should not be seen as absolute rules; they fail to factor in variables such as wind chill and velocity, levels of moisture in the soil and frost penetration. One night of, say, –20°C (–4°F) in the middle of winter will be unlikely to penetrate root systems of dormant perennials, but three nights would—and frost will be more damaging to wet soils than to those with better drainage. In short, while the lists below can be used as a rough guide to which plants may work in your garden, chances are that you will find advice from a local expert to be a much more helpful resource.

USDA Hardiness Zones	Equivalent UK Conditions
zone 1: below –46°C (–50°F)	–
zone 2: –46 to –40°C (–50 to –40°F)	–
zone 3: –40 to –34°C (–40 to –30°F)	–
zone 4: –34 to –29°C (–30 to –20°F)	–
zone 5: –29 to –23°C (–20 to –10°F)	hardy throughout most of the UK in areas where winter minimum is –24 to –20°C (–10 to –5°F).
zone 6: –23 to –18°C (–10 to 0°F)	hardy in most low elevations, provided there is some shelter and winter minimum of –18°C (0°F).
zone 7: –18 to –12°C (0 to 10°F)	hardy in sheltered areas where winter minimum is –15°C (5°F).
zone 8: –12 to –7°C (10 to 20°F)	hardy only in the most sheltered areas of the UK where the winter minimum is –12°C (10°F).
zone 9: –7 to –1°C (20 to 30°F)	requires cool glasshouse protection if temperature falls below –7°C (20°F).
zone 10: –1 to 4°C (30 to 40°F)	requires glasshouse conditions.
zone 11: above 4°C (40°F)	–

From Michael W. Buffin, *Winter-flowering Shrubs* (Timber Press, 2005).

Suppliers of Perennials and Grasses

United Kingdom

Ashwood Nurseries Ltd.
Ashwood Lower Lane
Ashwood, Kingswinford
West Midlands DY6 0AE
www.ashwoodnurseries.com

Beeches Nursery
Village Centre
Ashdon, Saffron Walden
Essex CB10 2HB
www.beechesnursery.co.uk

Beth Chatto Gardens Ltd.
Elmstead Market
Colchester
Essex CO7 7DB
www.bethchatto.co.uk

Binny Plants
West Lodge, Binny Estate
Ecclesmachen Road, Nr. Broxbourne
West Lothian EH52 6NL
Scotland
www.binnyplants.co.uk

Bressingham Gardens
Bressingham, Diss
Norfolk IP22 2AG
www.bressinghamgardens.com

Claire Austin Hardy Plants
Edgebolton
Shawbury, Shrewsbury
Shropshire SY4 4EL
www.claireaustin-hardyplants.co.uk

Cotswold Garden Flowers
Sands Lane
Badsey, Evesham
Worcestershire WR11 7EZ
www.cgf.net

Elizabeth MacGregor
Ellenbank
Kircudbright DG6 4UU
Scotland
www.elizabethmacgregor.co.uk

Hardy's Cottage Garden Plants
Priory Lane Nursery
Freefolk Priors, Whitchurch
Hampshire RG28 7NJ
www.hardys-plants.co.uk

Hillview Hardy Plants
Worfield, Nr. Bridgenorth
Shropshire WV15 5NT
www.hillviewhardyplants.com

Hopleys Plants
High Street, Much Hadham
Hertfordshire SG10 6BU
www.hopleys.co.uk

Knoll Gardens
Hampreston
Stapehill, Nr. Wimborne
Dorset BH21 7ND
www.knollgardens.co.uk

Long Acre Plants
South Marsh
Charlton Musgrove, Nr. Wincanton
Somerset BA9 8EX
www.plantsforshade.co.uk

Old Court Nurseries
Colwall, Nr. Malvern
Worcestershire WR13 6QE
www.autumnasters.co.uk

Park Green Nurseries
Wetheringsett, Stowmarket
Suffolk IP14 5QH
www.parkgreen.co.uk

The Plantsman's Preference
Lynwood, Hopton Road
Garboldisham, Diss
Norfolk IP22 2QN
www.plantpref.co.uk

The Wisley Plant Centre
R.H.S. Garden, Wisley
Woking
Surrey GU23 6QB
www.rhs.org.uk/wisleyplantcentre

Europe

Arends Maubach
Monschaustrasse 76
42369 Wuppertal–Ronsdorf
Germany
www.arends-maubach.de

Osnabrucker Staudenkulturen
Peter and Barbel zur Linden
Linner Kirchweg 2
D-49143 Bissendorf-Linne
Germany
www.zur-linden-stauden.de

Foerster Stauden GmbH
Am Raubfang 6
14469 Potsdam-Bornim
Germany
www.foerster-stauden.de

Coen Jansen Vaste Planten
Ankummer Es 13a
7722 RD Dalfsen
The Netherlands
www.coenjansenvasteplanten.nl

De Hessenhof
Hessenweg 41
6718 TC Ede
The Netherlands
www.hessenhof.nl

Nursery. Th. Ploeger en Zn. bv.
Blauwkapelseweg 73
3731 EB De Bilt
The Netherlands
www.ploegerdebilt.nl

Clos du Coudray
14 Rue du Parc Floral
76850 Etaimpuis, Normandy
France
www.closducoudray.com

Lepage Nurseries
Rue des Perrins
49130 Les-Ponts-de-Cé
France
www.lepage-vivaces.com

Poul Petersen
Overdam Nursery
Agiltevej 11
DK 2970 Hoersholm
Denmark
www.overdam.dk

Anne Stine Stauder
Obrovej 2
4295 Stenlille v/Soro
Denmark
www.annestinestauder.dk

North America

Arrowhead Alpines
1310 N. Gregory Road
P.O. Box 857
Fowlerville, Michigan
48836 USA
www.arowheadalpines.com

Fairweather Gardens
P.O. Box 333
Greenwich, New Jersey
08323 USA
www.fairweathergardens.com

Klehm's Song Sparrow Perennial
Farm
13101 East Rye Rd
Avalon, Wisconsin
53505 USA
www.songsparrow.com

Joy Creek Nursery
20300 NW Watson Road
Scappoose, Oregon
97956 USA
www.joycreek.com

Niche Gardens
1111 Dawson Road
Chapel Hill, North Carolina
27516 USA
www.nichegardens.com

Plant Delights Nursery
9241 Sauls Road
Ralcigh, North Carolina
27603 USA
www.plantdelights.com

Prairie Nursery
P.O. Box 306
Westfield, Wisconsin
53964 USA
www.prairienursery.com

Viette Farm and Nursery
P.O. Box 1109
State Route 608
Fishersville, Virginia
22939 USA
www.inthegardenradio.com

White Flower Farm
P.O. Box 50
Litchfield, Connecticut
06759 USA
www.whiteflowerfarm.com

References

Armitage, Allan M. *Herbaceous Perennial Plants*. Athens, GA: Varsity Press, 1989.

Armitage, Allan M. *Armitage's Garden Perennials*. Portland, OR: Timber Press, 2000.

Bendtsen, Birgitte Husted. *Phlox*. Denmark: Forlaget Geranium, 2007.

Bloom, Alan. *Alan Bloom's Hardy Perennials*. London: B. T. Batsford, 1991.

Campbell-Culver, Maggie. *The Origin of Plants*. London: Headline Book Publishing, 2000.

Carter, Susan, Carrie Becker and Bob Lilly. *Perennials*. Portland, OR: Timber Press, 2007.

Darke, Rick. *The American Woodland Garden*. Portland, OR: Timber Press, 2002.

Darke, Rick. *The Encyclopedia of Grasses for Livable Landscapes*. Portland, OR: Timber Press, 2007.

Disabato-Aust, Tracy. *The Well-Tended Perennial Garden*. Portland, OR: Timber Press, 1998.

Greenlee, John. *The Encyclopedia of Ornamental Grasses*. New York: Michael Friedman/Rodale Press, 1992.

Grounds, Roger. *Ornamental Grasses*. Newton Abbot, England: David and Charles, 1998.

Harper, Pamela J. *Time-Tested Plants*. Portland, OR: Timber Press, 2000.

Jellitto, Leo and Wilhelm Schacht. *Hardy Herbaceous Perennials*, vols I–II. London: B.T. Batsford, 1990.

Jones, Samuel B. and Leonard E. Foote. *Gardening with Native Wildflowers*. Portland, OR: Timber Press, 1990.

Mackenzie, David S. *Perennial Ground Covers*. Portland, OR: Timber Press, 1997.

Oliver, Charles and Martha. *Heuchera, Tiarella and Heucherella*. London: B. T. Batsford, 2006.

Picton, Paul. *Asters*. Newton Abbot, England: David and Charles and Portland, OR: Timber Press, 1999.

Rice, Graham (ed). *RHS Encyclopedia of Perennials*. London: Dorling Kindersley, 2006.

Rickett, Harold William. *Wildflowers of the United States*. New York: McGraw-Hill, 1965.

RHS Plant Finder, several editions until 2009/2010. London: Royal Horticultural Society/Dorling Kindersley, 2009.

Symons-Jeune, B. H. B. *Phlox*. London: Collins, 1954.

Thomas, Graham Stuart. *Perennial Garden Plants*. London: J. M. Dent, 1990.

Index of Plant Names

Page numbers in *italics* refer to photographs.

Acknowledgements

First and foremost I would like to thank my wife Rosemary and our youngest son Richard. 'Rosie' was with me from start to finish, interpreting my handwriting and, with helpful suggestions, typing the manuscript. Richard ('Rich') not only travelled widely and to many gardens to take wonderful pictures, but also helped me to reduce several thousand images to two hundred, perhaps time which could have been more profitably used elsewhere in our photo library business.

Thanks to Gary Doerr, President of Blooms of Bressingham and to Joe Kunkel, prime organizer for the larger gardens, who both have supported and encouraged my efforts to promote, through the giveaway garden scheme, a wider interest in plants and gardening in North America.

And to my editor Erica Gordon-Mallin thanks for her patience and professionalism in producing a book so close to my aims, despite lively debates as to how to cut eleven thousand words from my original text.

Rich and I, who between us visited all of the gardens portrayed in this book, would like to thank the owners for allowing us to do so: Royal Horticultural Society Wisley, Richard Ayres, Mark Rumary, Tom Stuart-Smith, Sir Charles and Lady Legard of Scampston Hall, Dennis Schrader and Bill Smith, Judy and Malcolm Pearce, Keith and Ros Wiley, Rick Darke, Paul Picton, James and Jan Saunt, Jan and Sabine zu Jeddeloh, Cassian Schmidt of Hermanshof, Jean le Bret, Pamela Harper, Tim and Isabella Vaughan, Bill Thomas of Chanticleer Garden, Maggie and Steve Putt, Roy and Judy Johnson.